THE WINDOW OF CHRISTIANITY

Reframing Pandemic

In *Reframing Pandemic* Dr. Bob Keay offers an inspiring, masterful
and eminently readable overview of the grand Biblical narrative
which highlights its relevance to the coronavirus pandemic, and
more generally to the way believers understand the role of science
and medicine. The book synthesises insights from the fields of
biblical studies, archaeology, church history and virology to tell the
story of God's and humanity's involvement with creation from the
dawn of time, to the work of Christ, to the present, and finally to
the climax of history. The story is enchanting and hope inducing, a
must for anyone interested in understanding theologically our
world.

Dr. Charlie Hadjiev
Lecturer in Old Testament and Hebrew,
Queen's University, Belfast and Belfast Bible College

At first I thought, "reframing pandemic? What's that?" Then I read
and it made perfect sense. Sweeping from past to future, from
Genesis to Apocalypse, Keay's well documented essay reveals the
big picture. Once reframed, the virus fits well into a larger biblical
pattern. The current situation is not surprising, but it is not
hopeless either. You will look at the pandemic through new glasses.

Dr. Antoine Bret
Associate Professor of Plasma Physics,
Universidad Castilla-La Mancha.
Visiting Scholar,
Harvard-Smithsonian Center for Astrophysics

THE WINDOW OF CHRISTIANITY

Reframing Pandemic

Robert Keay

BP
Basiliad Publishing

Reframing Pandemic
Series Title: *The Window of Christianity*
Printed in the USA.
Published by KDP in cooperation with Basiliad Publishing.
For information contact the author at rkeayjr@gmail.com.

Cover design by Joshua Keay.
Cover painting: *The Plague in Rome*. Italy, 17th century.
Rome, Museo Storico Nazionale Dell'Arte Sanitaria

"The purpose of medicine is to relieve suffering;
of religion to explain suffering or to help us accept it."

Anonymous

CONTENTS

ACKNOWLEDGMENTS

This short book began life as a sermon titled "God, the Pandemic, and You" preached for the Sharon Congregational Church on 15 March 2020, the last Sunday before closing the sanctuary due to the coronavirus pandemic. Closing the building opened the church to exploring and experimenting with new ways of being church and exercising ministry. This book emerged during those days as an attempt to situate the pandemic in the larger Christian story, and therefore to provide hope and confidence in a better day to come. I am thankful to the congregation for their support throughout this difficult time. I appreciate the endorsements from my former colleague in Belfast Dr. Charlie Hadjiev and my new friend Dr. Antoine Bret, who shares a scholarly interest in the relationship between science and faith. Thanks are due to Joshua Keay for his cover design and early advice regarding direction and content. Colin Bovaird read and edited the manuscript with great care and improved it significantly. My wife, Jill Gamble, also provided expert editorial advice throughout the process, as well as much needed encouragement. Perhaps most importantly, Jill brings lightness and joy as we journey through life together, and I am pleased to dedicate this work to her.

INTRODUCTION

The purpose of this book is to examine the coronavirus pandemic through lenses offered by Christianity. The book is the first in a series titled *The Window of Christianity*. This window, Christianity, I will argue, provides a helpful way of reframing the pandemic. Hence the title of the book, *Reframing Pandemic*. By looking through the window of Christianity, we see the pandemic in a much broader frame, and one which offers an optimistic perspective and a motivational impulse. We plan to reframe other contemporary matters through the window of Christianity in future issues in the series. A few definitions and explanations are needed before we proceed.

When I speak of Christianity, I am referring to the comprehensive story of Jesus Christ told in the Bible, rather than the history of the Christian church or of Christians, their practices and behaviors, on the ground around the globe. That literary story about Jesus Christ is comprehensive in that I see its beginnings at the start of Genesis and its conclusion at the end of Revelation. Thus, the Christianity that I speak of is a grand narrative that begins with the creation of the world and concludes with a restoration of the world, and which is centered on the life of the man Jesus Christ. I am not suggesting, however, that this literary expression of Christianity is unrelated to the real world and events that occur in our lives. I claim that this literary Christianity invades the real world and motivates real world activity in important historical intersections, primarily in the life of Jesus and those who continue his project. This grand narrative provides a window on the world, enabling us to look at contemporary matters in its frame, and allowing us to evaluate our response to those matters in terms set by Jesus. Developing this metaphor further, the window of Christianity consists of many smaller panes through which we look at the particular matters of life. Those smaller panes are the individual biblical stories and texts that make up the whole narrative.

In order to reframe the coronavirus pandemic in the window of Christianity, I will be focusing primarily on the view through three panes: those at the beginning (Genesis 1-11), the end (Revelation 21-22), and the center or turning point of the narrative (Gospels). These panes provide the fundamental plotline of the grand narrative.

In Part I, "Alpha & Omega", I consider the panes at the beginning and end of the grand narrative, and demonstrate how they work together to reframe the coronavirus pandemic in a realistic and optimistic way. The beginning pane reveals that God's purpose in creating is to see life flourish and thrive (Genesis 1-2). The end pane reveals the striking success of God's plan. The whole of creation thrives with life (Revelation 21-22). Admittedly such texts are visionary and idealistic and lack the necessary concrete historical grounding to elicit such optimistic confidence. We do recognize our situation, however, when the initial vision turns bleak as sin, evil, destruction, and death invade and permeate the world. Such a realistic picture of our world only magnifies the distance between the optimistic framing panes. The next part solves this problem with an historical bridge.

In Part II, "Bridging Alpha & Omega", I consider the pane at the center of the narrative, the story of Jesus, and how it links the panes at the beginning and end in real history. In this pane we see Jesus, embodying God's love for the world, inaugurating an historical project of reclaiming and restoring the world for God. The older idealistic visions appear to have inspired and propelled him on his mission. The success of his mission is seen in the concrete historical acts described by those who wrote his story. These acts, demonstrating his power over illness and nature, and culminating in his death, resurrection, and ascension, persuaded many that God was indeed reclaiming and restoring the world through the mission of Jesus. His followers, full of hope and optimism, confidently continued the mission and spread his teachings and practices around the world. They embodied Christ's selfless and sacrificial love for humanity and spread the good news that he is progressively remaking humanity and the world. That same mission continues and progresses today, giving us hope that the coronavirus will ultimately be eradicated from the earth, just as smallpox has been, and that we are indeed on a path toward the new creation.

The book is an exercise in what might be called pastoral theology in biblical-narrative mode. It is not an apologetic for Christianity. I make no attempt to argue for the truth of the biblical grand narrative that frames the pandemic. It is not a theodicy. It is an effort to integrate the pandemic into a biblical narrative that tells the story of God's plan for humanity and his world. The goal of the work is to provide hope and motivate action. Seen through the window of Christianity, the coronavirus pandemic is a temporary eruption of the dangerous powers of a world disturbed by human abuses. How long the pandemic goes on depends on humanity's response to it. God has given humans the responsibility to subdue and harness the powers of the natural world. He has given the gifts necessary to accomplish that task—intelligence, creativity, the desire to work cooperatively. And most importantly, he has already effected the reordering of the virus through the accomplishments of Jesus Christ. All that remains is for humans to follow through on the work he initiated and bring it to its conclusion. Scientists and health care workers are God's frontline soldiers in this effort, and they must be supported in every way by everyone. This is how God has designed his world to work.

Alpha & Omega

CONSPECTUS OF PART I

Part I explores texts at the very beginning and very end of the grand narrative, thereby revealing the goal toward which the story of Christianity is heading. Looking through these two panes in the window of Christianity offers us hope that the coronavirus pandemic is temporary and will be eradicated. God began a good work in creation (Genesis 1-2) and He will complete that work someday in the future (Revelation 21-22).

In chapter 1, "Alpha: Creation Good but Not Safe", we consider the story of creation as told in Genesis 1-11. From texts in Genesis 1-2 we discover that the "goodness" of creation consists in its dynamic potential to display the magnificence of God when it flourishes under the governing hand of humans—bearers of the divine image. We also learn that the creation is "not safe" because it requires its governing authority to domesticate or harness its potencies to achieve that goodness. God, who is mankind's sovereign authority, appoints humanity to govern the creation. From texts in Genesis 3-11 we see humanity repudiate God's authority, and consequently fail in their governance of the creation. The resultant disharmony in the relationship between God and humanity is mirrored in the disharmony amongst humans and in the disruptions in the natural world.

In chapter 2, "Pandemic: Creation Broken and Deadly", we consider the place of viruses and the coronavirus in the world. We learn that viruses are "good" because they enable the diversity of life to flourish on the earth, but they can become deadly when they migrate to hosts not prepared to accept them. The coronavirus is a particularly deadly virus and requires the cooperative efforts of all humans to respond to it appropriately. Science is making progress in understanding viruses and the coronavirus in particular, but we are still in the beginning stages of research and knowledge.

In chapter 3 we consider texts that describe the recreation of the world at the end of the Christian narrative. Here we find that the destructive and deadly powers of the creation will one day be reordered and governed properly so as to fulfill their purpose of displaying the beauty and glory of God. Thus, according to the grand narrative, humanity will someday reign over a world in which viruses live commensally with their hosts and life flourishes beautifully.

1

ALPHA
Creation Good but Not Safe

Introduction

Genesis 12 begins Israel's story. God calls Abram to leave his home in Ur of the Chaldees and travel to another land that God will show him. God promises to give him a son and make him into a great nation that will bless all peoples on the earth (Genesis 12.1-3). The rest of the Bible is the story of the children of Abram, later renamed Abraham, and how they become the children of Israel, chosen to serve God as "a light to the nations" (Isaiah 42.6; 49.6), and ultimately how they fulfill God's promise to bless all people through their Messiah-King, Jesus. But the Bible does not begin at Genesis 12. Genesis 1-11 provides the necessary pre-history that explains why God called Abram and why all people need God's blessing. Genesis 1-2 explains that God created the world and gave humanity responsibility to govern that world. Genesis 3-11 explains that humanity failed to govern the world in accordance with God's design and instead disordered and corrupted the design of the world and set it on a path to destruction. Genesis 12, then, introduces Abram as God's choice to begin the process of rescuing the world from its corruption and impending destruction.

The story told in Genesis 1-11 is fundamental, then, for establishing Israel's self-identity and divinely given vocation. Israel is the people whom God chose to repair the world. During times of national crisis—such as in the sixth-century BCE, when the nation was ruthlessly overthrown, Jerusalem and the temple destroyed, and the people taken captive to Babylon—the prophets returned to this primeval narrative to reassess and reorient the nation's identity and vocation. Isaiah and Jeremiah found in this narrative an explanation for the crisis, as well as hope for a future restoration (e.g., Isaiah 40; Jeremiah 4). The narrative provided both critique and hope for the people. It reframed their situation and gave them valuable wisdom to respond effectively. It encouraged them to believe that God had not forsaken them, but would fulfill his plans through a faithful remnant. Later, the Apostle Paul returned to that same narrative for help in understanding the great crisis of first-century Israel, the crucifixion of the messianic king (Romans 5.12-21 and 1 Corinthians 15.20-22).

This same creation narrative can provide help today to understand the crisis that now confronts us. The coronavirus pandemic confronts the world with critical questions about humanity's failures and hopes. How are we to understand such a catastrophe? How can we believe that God is good in the face of such suffering and death? Should we believe that God will rescue his world? Should we simply accept that this is the way life is, and that trying to find meaning and hope is pointless and absurd? We will follow the example of the ancient prophets and apostles and turn to the primeval narrative to see what help it offers in reframing this crisis and guiding us toward a positive response.

The Creation is Good

Prior to God's creative words being spoken (i.e., "Let there be light", etc.), we are told that "the earth was without form and void and darkness was over the face of the deep" (1.2). God then speaks and gives form to the formlessness, fills the void, and illumines the darkness (1.3-31). This story of creation is told in a six day sequence. On days 1-3 God forms the earth, arranging, organizing, and shaping the contours of land, sea, and sky (1.3-13); then, on days 4-6, God fills those large empty places with sun, moon and stars, and fish, birds, and animals, and finally with humans (1.14-31). Created reality is given by God, and it is good. At points along the way we are repeatedly told that "God saw that it was good" (1.4, 10, 12, 18, 21, 25). This creation story comes to a climax with the statement "And God saw everything that he had made, and behold, it was very good" (1.31). God transformed a formless and void chaos into a beautiful and harmonious cosmos. The text explains in more detail what is meant by the goodness of the creation. We will consider first the goodness of humanity and then the goodness of the earth.

The Goodness of Humanity

On the sixth day God created humanity—male and female—in his own image. That they are created in God's image reveals their uniqueness in all of creation. As God is creative, so humans also possess imagination and creativity; as God seeks to relate to others, so humans also possess a desire for relationship and cooperation. Humans reflect the presence of this creative and relational God in the world. It is for this reason that humans are given dominion over the natural realm. Humanity's stewardship over the natural realm is the logical follow-up to their being created in the image of God. As God rules over all reality, so His image-bearers rule in their designated domain, earth.

> Then God said, "Let us make man in our image, after our likeness. And let them have dominion of the fish of the sea and over the birds of the sky and over the livestock and over all the earth and over everything that creeps on the earth." So God created man in his own image. In the image of God he created him; male and female he created them. And God blessed them. And God said to them, "Be fruitful and multiply and fill the earth and subdue it, and have dominion over the fish of the sea, the birds of the sky, and over every living thing that moves on the earth." (Genesis 1.26-28)

When we consider the "goodness" of humanity, it is evident that "goodness" must refer primarily to humanity's unique responsibility of reflecting the image of God in the creation and their consequential dominion over that creation. God entrusted humanity with the responsibility to govern or steward ("have dominion of") the earth and all living things. He therefore endowed them with the intellectual capacity necessary to accomplish this task, as well as with the relational instincts and desires required for success. These divine-like qualities are intrinsic or inherent in humanity; they define what it means to be human, and they enable humanity to function well in God's world. Humans are naturally gifted and suited to serve as God's partners in the governance of the creation. And they are given clear instructions on how to proceed: Populate the earth, subdue it, and govern it (1.28).

Genesis 2 offers a re-telling of the story of humanity's creation and vocation, with additional emphases. We read:

> When no bush of the field was yet in the land and no small plant of the field had yet sprung up—for the Lord God had not caused it to rain on the land, and there was no human to cultivate the ground— . . . then the Lord God formed the man of dust from the ground and breathed into his nostrils the breath of life. The Lord God planted a garden in the east, in Eden, and there he put the man whom he had formed. . . . The Lord God took the man and put him in the garden to cultivate and guard it. (Genesis 2.5, 7-8, 15)

This text emphasizes that God created the man to work cooperatively with the natural realm in order to enable the earth to realize its productive potential. The earth needs both rain and human hands in order to flourish. The text then states that it was "not good" for the man to be alone in this vocation; he needed a helper (2.18). So God created all kinds of animals, but none were deemed suitable to take on this vocation (2.19-20). So God put the man to sleep, took flesh from the man, and reshaped it into a woman (2.21-25). Humanity was now complete and fully furnished to accomplish its vocation of governing the world. Only humanity, male and female, made in the image of God, is capable of succeeding in this divinely given vocation. They must work in harmony with each other and in cooperation with the design of the natural realm. In so doing they are working in cooperation with the Creator God and reflecting his image throughout creation.

The Goodness of the Earth

Having found that the text identifies the goodness of humanity with their creation in the image of God and consequentially with their divinely given vocation to serve God as stewards of his creation, we can now consider the "goodness" of the earth and the whole realm of nature. We must be careful not to import alien concepts of goodness into the text, but to follow the text closely (Moberly 2009: 43, n.4). The concept can only be understood within the literary context of the story itself. Just as humanity's goodness was explained by the text, so too is nature's goodness. Clearly its goodness does not mean that it is unchangeable and static. It cannot mean that it is fully developed and flourishing. The story highlights the fact that there was much necessary work to be done by humans in the cultivation of the natural order (2.5). Its goodness means it is prepared to be cultivated and will respond productively when it is cultivated well; that is, it is fit for purpose; it is ready to exercise its fertility for good. Westermann says, "it is good or suited for the purpose for which it is being prepared; it corresponds to its goal" (1971: 61). It is pregnant with the potential to enable life to proliferate and prosper. The author describes such God-given intrinsic potencies in the natural realm:

> And God said, "Let the earth sprout vegetation, plants yielding seed, and fruit trees bearing fruit in which is their seed, each according to its kind, on the earth." And it was so. The earth brought forth vegetation, plants yielding seed according to their own kinds, and trees bearing fruit in which is their seed, each according to its kind. And God saw that it was good.
> (Genesis 1.11-12)

> And God said, "Let the earth bring forth living creatures according to their kinds: livestock and creeping things and beasts of the earth, according to their kinds." And it was so.
> (Genesis 1.24)

Nahum Sarna (1989: 8) writes, "God endows it [earth] with generative powers that He now activates by His utterance." Thus, the earth is divinely empowered to enable a multitude of life forms to flourish and thrive in it. Just as humans are created with inherent capacities (intellectual and relational qualities) to fulfill their role in the world, so too the natural realm is created with inherent tendencies to impel it toward the fulfillment of its purposes; this is the essence of its goodness. By divine design the earth sprouts and brings forth vegetation; plants yield seeds; and seeds bear fruit. Rain and human hands contribute within the divine design to bring the world to its intended goal.

The Creation is Not Safe

Some of these natural forces in the earth are necessarily extremely powerful. The cosmos is an ordering of massive powers that, if disordered, threaten the life forms it supports. Such powerful forces are necessary to maintain an environment that sustains life —gravity and magnetism sustain its cosmic stability, winds blow across its surface to regulate its temperature, massive tectonic plates shift to allow minerals forged at its core to rise to the surface for use by humans as tools, and seas churn with powerful waves to nourish marine life. These dynamic forces are both life-enabling and life-threatening. Water, in which life abounds, can drown land-dwelling creatures; flood waters can either wreak chaos or be channeled to irrigate crops. Earthquakes, and hurricanes, and volcanoes may provide minerals, nourish soil, and cleanse the atmosphere, but they can also endanger the lives of humans unprepared for their powerful eruptions. These are all good, but dangerous. Earthquakes are no more evil because they can endanger life than the sea is evil because it can drown. They are fit for purpose, but their powers must be controlled, harnessed, and channeled toward beneficial ends. If disorder prevails the cosmos will return to chaos and death.

Humanity Appointed as Stewards

The nature of the cosmos as good but not safe meant it needed intelligent and good stewards to cultivate its goodness and harness its dangerous powers. Therefore, God appointed humanity as its stewards or governors. He instructed them to "subdue" the earth.

To "subdue" is to harness or control a power. For example, the word is used to describe an army taking control of an enemy military force (2 Samuel 8.11). When the Israelites crossed the Jordan River to dwell in the land promised to them, it was necessary that they "subdue" any opposing inhabitants (Numbers 32.22, 29; Joshua 18.1; 1 Chronicles 22.18). When hostile forces are subdued, they can be harnessed and channeled for beneficial ends. After subduing an enemy army, victors often profit from the "spoils" of war; likewise, after subduing the forces of nature, humans profit by the natural energy and productive capacities they offer. Domesticating animals, such as the ox, harnesses power for agricultural service.

God also instructed humans to "cultivate and guard" the earth (2.15). The agricultural import of these words is clearly illustrated by the need for a man to "cultivate the ground" in 2.5 (cf. 3.23). The inherent powers of the natural world must be directed, pruned, and guided by the intelligence of humanity. But this metaphor goes beyond agriculture, and recognizes that the earth provides many and varied resources to build human culture, society, and civilization, and that all of these need to be wisely and carefully cultivated and guarded. Interestingly, the choice of these two words (cultivate and guard) may be a deliberate allusion to the priestly service in the tabernacle. These words are often found in such contexts, where they are typically translated "serve and guard" with reference to the priests' service for God in the sanctuary (Numbers 3.7-8; 8.25-26; 18.5-6; cf. 1 Chronicles 23.32). If this is a deliberate allusion, the significance appears to be that man's cultivating and guarding the earth is comparable to the priests' service to God in the tabernacle. And this may suggest that the created realm is the place where God and humans are meant to dwell together as in a sanctuary (cf. Genesis 3.8). Furthermore, the choice of these words emphasizes that humans are subordinate to God in their work, and that what is required of them is faithfulness and obedience in their service as stewards.

That humans are given responsibility to cultivate the earth indicates its productive potential for greater good; that humans are given responsibility to guard it indicates its fragility and potential for disintegration; and that humans are given responsibility to subdue it indicates its dangerous qualities and potential to harm, as well as its dynamic potential for good when its powers are properly harnessed. To subdue the earth meant that its massive powers had to be controlled and channeled for the benefit of humanity and to mitigate the dangers it presented. To cultivate the created order meant that it possessed the seed of something more wondrous. The partnership of God and His human stewards was meant to produce something truly wonderful. The Psalmist, meditating upon these truths, wonders at the awesome privilege given to mere humans:

> What is man that you are mindful of him,
> The son of man that you care for him?
> You have made him a little lower than the angels,
> And crowned him with glory and honor.
> You have given him dominion over the works of your hands;
> You have put all things under his feet.
> (Psalm 8.4-6)

We must add, however, that human responsibility to cultivate the earth does not mean that humans are free to exercise their imagination and authority in any way they please. The whole story of humanity's creation in the image of God and calling to serve as stewards of God is framed within the story of God's creation of the entire cosmic order, and evaluating it as good. Thus, humans must obey the Sovereign Creator's instructions, and work with the inherent design of nature. Sarna (1989: 12-13) emphasizes these two realities:

> The human race is not inherently sovereign, but enjoys its dominion solely by the grace of God. . . . Moreover, man, the sovereign of nature, is conceived at this stage to be functioning within the context of a "very good" world in which the interrelationships of organisms with their environment and with each other are entirely harmonious and mutually beneficial, an idyllic situation that is clearly illustrated in Isaiah's vision of the ideal future king (Isa. 11.1-9).

Creation is a given reality, designed and ordered carefully to enable life to flourish. Humanity must exercise its stewardship within the boundaries of this given reality and in accordance with its inherent design and intention. Given the nature of reality, there will be much room for diversity and imagination and creativity; nevertheless, there are established boundaries and goals, and these must be recognized and respected. Humans must cooperate with the given reality in order to be successful, as Genesis 2.5 made clear. While this truth is evident in the natural realm, as farmers know well, it is also true in every other aspect of life in the world God created.

Thus, we see in Genesis 1-2 that God created a world full of potency, and gave humanity the responsibility to cultivate its potential for good, to guard it against potential losses, and to subdue its potential for harm and channel it for good. He created humans in relationship with one another, to work in concert with each other, and to work cooperatively with the natural realm. He gave them the intellectual curiosity and the imaginative creativity to construct that world full of beauty and diversity. All of this was "very good" (1.31). But the author of Genesis 1-2 knew that he did not live in that world, and that there was something terribly wrong with humanity and the world. Genesis 3-11 is his attempt to explain what is wrong with the world he lived in.

Humanity Disorders the Cosmic Order

We have seen from Genesis 2.15 that God formed the man and put him into the garden to cultivate and guard it. God then invited the man to eat freely from all the trees in the garden (2.16), except for one tree that possessed the power to kill the man—the tree of the knowledge of good and evil (2.17). God is described here as generous and protective of the man, highlighting both the benefits and dangers in the creation. Genesis 3 continues this part of the story, but takes the narrative in a different direction.

In Genesis 3 an alien element is introduced—one of the animals God created, a serpent, is engaged in conversation with the woman, attempting to persuade her of his alternative vision of the world. In the serpent's reconstructed view God is portrayed as miserly, untrustworthy, and selfish; God's generosity and desire to protect the man and the woman are turned upside-down.

Now the serpent was more crafty than any other wild animal that the Lord God had made. He said to the woman, "Did God say, 'You shall not eat from any tree in the garden?'" The woman said to the serpent, "We may eat of the fruit of the trees in the garden, but God said, 'You shall not eat of the fruit of the tree that is in the middle of the garden, nor shall you touch it, or you shall die.'" But the serpent said to the woman, "You will not die, for God knows that when you eat of it your eyes will be opened, and you will be like God, knowing good and evil." So when the woman saw that the tree was good for food, and that it was a delight to the eyes, and that the tree was to be desired to make one wise, she took of its fruit and ate. And she gave some to her husband who was with her and he ate. Then the eyes of both were opened, and they knew that they were naked, and they sewed fig leaves together and made loincloths for themselves.
(Genesis 3.1-7)

The author makes no attempt to explain the origin of the serpent, other than that he is one of God's creatures, or to explain the reasons for the serpent's contrary nature. The point of the story is that the man and the woman were responsible to guard the garden, to protect it from harm, and to exercise authority over the animals, including this sly one. However, confronted by a crafty animal with a subtle argument, the humans fail in their God-given vocation and are persuaded to live within the serpent's alternative vision of reality. That alternative perspective appealed to their intellectual curiosity, their aesthetic appreciation, and their agricultural responsibility, but it contradicted God's instructions.

They saw that the fruit was good for food, aesthetically beautiful, and intellectually beneficial, so they ate, despite having been warned of its dangers. They opened pandora's box. They inaugurated a fundamental disordering of the cosmos. The alternative version of reality was a destructive lie with immediate consequences. Eating from the tree introduced death into the world, just as God had warned. Relationships broke down (3.8-13) and the world began to fall apart (3.14-19). The man and woman turned against each other and against God. They turned inward. They hid from God and blamed each other. The good world, now disordered, was on a path toward chaos and death.

Humanity had allowed its own innate gifts to override its vocation as stewards responsible to God. They failed to subdue and harness their own powers and desires. The story presents a lesson for humanity in its approach to governing the earth and constructing human society, culture, and civilizations. While intellectual curiosity and creative imagination are necessary to fulfill the call to cultivate the earth, these gifts must be exercised in harmony with the reality of the God-given order. Alternative visions that contradict known reality necessarily bring chaos and death. Attempts to construct the world based on lies spell disaster. They are inherently unstable and will necessarily collapse.

Death and Destruction Spread Across the World

As the story unfolds in Genesis 4-11 we see humanity spreading across the globe, exercising its dominion in ways contrary to God's design, and therefore reaping the whirlwind. On an individual level, the failure to subdue strong human emotions results in murder.

God warns Cain, "sin is crouching at the door; its desire is against you; you must rule over it" (4.7), but Cain refuses to subdue his jealousy and murders Abel (4.8). Abel's blood cries out from the ground (4.10), and the ground itself turns against Cain and refuses to yield its powers to his cultivating work (4.12). The natural realm and the spiritual realm are a unity. This unity is seen most dramatically in the flood story. Humanity's recalcitrance incites a devastating deluge (Genesis 6-9). Failure to live in harmony with reality brings disaster.

Genesis 6, 10 and 11 describe another consequence of humanity exercising their dominion without regard to God's design for the world. Human society, culture, and civilization become dominated by power rather than truth and reality. Human selfishness and greed dominate the practice of ruling, rather than service and care to others. Oppressive and exploitative regimes are born. Genesis 6 and 10 tell of "mighty men", "men of renown" who built empires through abuse and injustice. Nimrod was the first mighty man. His empire began in Babel, the land of Shinar (Babylonia), and extended to Assyria and its main city Nineveh (10.8-12). The Assyrian and the Babylonian empires would become the great enemies of Israel and Judah and the cause of their downfall and captivity. Nevertheless, despite their power and wealth, these empires are doomed to collapse and fail. Their own downfall is sure, as the prophets announce, and as Genesis 11 portends with the story of the tower of Babel.

This concluding story tells of humanity organizing in rebellion against God's designs for the world. God sees how powerful these mighty men have become—"nothing shall be impossible for them" (11.6), but he then reveals the consequences of a civilization built on lies by confusing their language and dispersing them over the face of the earth (11.7-9). With this story, the narrative concludes. Humanity has become powerful and they use their power to construct the world according to their own selfish designs. They exercise their God-given vocation by creating the world as they desire it to be rather than in harmony with its God-designed reality. The consequence of their broken relationships is a plethora of competing visions and agendas. Unless they can be rescued, they will destroy themselves and the whole creation. Babel or Babylon will henceforth be the epitome of evil in the biblical narrative. The story of Babylon continues to the end of history, when, in the book of Revelation, Babylon becomes the epicenter of worldwide rebellion against God, and then surprisingly self-destructs as the nations allied to the city suddenly turn against the city and destroy it (Revelation 17.15-18).

Conclusion

We have said that Genesis 1-11 provides the necessary prelude to the story of Israel, explaining their identity and vocation as "a light to the nations" (Isaiah 42.6; 49.6), sent on a mission to rescue and restore a world heading for destruction and death. This window pane describes a world that is rich with potential to flourish with a brilliant diversity of life, but which also has the potential to threaten life if it is not harnessed and subdued. Humans are presented as wonderfully gifted by God to domesticate and cultivate the world for their own benefit and in display of God's glory. They choose to use those gifts, however, to construct the world according to their own self-aggrandizing plans and purposes. And in so doing they work against the design of the cosmos and instigate a deadly reaction from the cosmos. The cosmos turns against humanity and threatens its very existence. This story explains an inherent contradiction within the world. It is a world full of beauty and power, but also full of danger and death. It was created very good, but has been exploited and abused, and now exhibits great evils and is on a path toward destruction and death. The present state of the world, full of corruption and wickedness, is not the way it should be or was intended to be. This window pane offers us a way to view the coronavirus pandemic.

2

PANDEMIC
Creation Broken and Deadly

Introduction

Humanity was instructed to "be fruitful and multiply, fill the earth and subdue it, and have dominion" (Genesis 1.28). Humanity has fulfilled its first responsibility to God: populating the planet. Humans now cover the globe. That immense population puts a great burden on the planet to feed and sustain it. It can do so, but only with humanity's wise cultivating hand guiding it toward greater productivity. There are nearly 8 billion of us living on this earth. When my father was born in 1927 the world population had just reached 2 billion. When I was born in 1959 the number reached 3 billion. During my lifetime it has reached nearly 8 billion. Such remarkable growth increases the demand for food production. Yet the amount of arable land has been decreasing. Cities are spreading, and global warming is changing the climate. Soil erosion and pollution portend further dangers to agriculture. Humanity is faced with a great task to steward this world in order to make the planet habitable for these vast numbers.

The earth that humans inhabit is an interconnected network of interdependent living and non-living things. Its many habitats are deeply integrated and work in mutuality and reciprocity to sustain its life forms. We have learned much about the massive powers inherent in the planet—wind, waves, and tectonic plates. These powers are essential for life to flourish and thrive; nevertheless, they also pose dangers—hurricanes, tsunamis, volcanoes, and earthquakes. Humans are responsible for stewarding this planet, subduing these massive powers, and protecting and cultivating its life forms. Viruses are part of this network, and although small, they possess tremendous powers to influence the life of every creature on the planet, including humans.

Viruses and Virology

The story of humanity's attempts to understand viruses is a rather short one compared to other academic endeavors (see Zimmer 2015 for the full story). The story begins with scientists trying to understand the cause of mysterious contagious diseases such as small pox. The initial clue came in 1898 when Dr Martinus Beijerinck, working in his laboratory at Delft University of Technology, discovered the cause of a particular disease in tobacco plants. Beijerinck extracted liquid from the plant and put it through a porcelain filter. What emerged was an infectious agent, which Beijerinck called *contagium vivum fluidum*, which he later named "virus", Latin for "venom" or "poison." Shortly thereafter two German scientists demonstrated a similar filtered agent to be the cause of foot-and-mouth disease in cattle. Three years later, in 1901, Walter Reed, a US Army physician, identified the agent causing yellow fever in humans. Viruses had been discovered and the science of virology had begun.

With such a beginning it's no surprise that viruses do not have a good reputation. Viruses were typically defined as infectious agents causing disease. In a standard work, *Viruses and Man*, written in 1955, Frank MacFarlane Burnet, 1960 recipient of a Nobel Prize for his work in immunology, wrote:

> We can define a virus then as a microorganism responsible for disease which is capable of growth only within the living cells of a susceptible host—and which is normally considered smaller than any bacterium.
> (cited from Pradeu 2016: 81)

For most of its history, researchers working in the discipline of virology were focused almost exclusively on understanding the relationship between viruses and infectious disease in order to find cures. Within the population at large the word virus conjures up stories of horrible diseases: HIV, ebola, the zika virus, and of course the flu. However, this negative reputation is changing, at least among virologists.

As the new academic field grew, more expansive and thorough-going studies led virologists to consider the possibility that viruses do more than cause disease. For example, in the late 1980s Lita Proctor, a graduate student at the State University of New York at Stony Brook, wanted to find out how many viruses are in sea water. There had never been a study of the topic, and most scientists had assumed there were very few. What Proctor discovered was astonishing. Her samples suggested there were as many as one hundred billion viruses in every liter of sea water! Other scientists joined the project and repeatedly confirmed these tremendous numbers (Zimmer 2015: 47-48). Professor Marilyn Roossinck (2016: 42) now says there are far more viruses in the ocean than there are stars in all the known galaxies. Researchers offer a rough estimate that there are 10,000,000,000,000,000,000,000,000,000,000 viruses in the ocean. If viruses are so plentiful, could they all be bad? At the end of the 20th century, in 1999, Paul Griffiths, a Professor of Virology at University College London, published an essay in *Reviews in Medical Virology* asking, "Is it time to consider the concept of a commensal virus?" He concluded rather tentatively, "We should not exclude the possibility that commensal viruses may exist."

Good Viruses

Just over twenty years later virology has been revolutionized by the discovery of many new viruses that not only do not harm their host, but are beneficial and even essential for the life of their host. New technologies in sequencing genes allow researchers to study these newly discovered viruses. Just as we now know that there are good bacteria, essential for intestinal health and well-being, so also we are now discovering that there are good viruses. The discipline has changed so dramatically in the last few decades, that there is no longer a consensus amongst virologists on the definition of a virus or even the essential nature of a virus. There is consensus, however, on the fact that viruses are the most abundant type of organism on earth, and that they are essential to all forms of life on earth. Mario Mietzsch and Mavis Agbandjie-McKenna report in the September 2017 *Annual Review of Virology*, "Our experience as virologists suggests that the use of 'good' viruses is common practice." They may be too small to see with the naked eye, but they play a fundamental role in the interconnected biosphere that we call home, and that we are responsible to subdue, cultivate, and guard as stewards.

Virologists now categorize viruses as pathogenic (harmful to their host) and nonpathogenic (not harmful to their host). The nonpathogenic far outnumber the pathogenic. In the nonpathogentic category, some viruses simply live harmoniously with their host, others provide a mutually beneficial service to their host, and some are essential for the life of their host. It is important to clarify that these categories describe particular functions of viruses within particular environments, not the nature of the virus itself. In regard to its basic nature a virus is neither good nor bad, but placed within a specific environment it can be either harmful, neutral, or helpful. It is therefore necessary that humans understand viruses and how they function within particular environments in order to harness their power for good and subdue their potential for harm. Influenza viruses are nonpathogenic in birds, but pathogenic in humans. The coronavirus is nonpathogenic in bats, but pathogenic in humans.

Scientists are also discovering that healthy humans are host to far more nonpathogenic viruses than ever imagined. In 1997 researchers in Japan discovered a new virus in the blood of humans, the torque tenovirus. Further study revealed that this virus belongs to the anelloviruses group and is extremely common throughout all human populations and has no negative effects in human hosts. In 2009 Dana Willner conducted tests on the microbial content of human lungs. Prior to the study it was thought that healthy human lungs were free of viruses. However, Willner discovered an average of 174 different viruses in her subjects, and 90% of these were completely new to scientists. A 2012 study on microbes found on human skin reports that

> The human skin is a complex ecosystem that hosts a heterogenous flora. . . . There are now many evidences that viruses represent a significant part of the cutaneous flora as demonstrated by the asymptomatic carriage of beta and gamma human papillomaviruses on the healthy skin. . . . The results emphasize the high diversity of the viral cutaneous flora with multiple polyomaviruses, papillomaviruses and circoviruses being detected on normal-appearing skin.
> (Foulongne 2012)

We now know that nonpathogenic viruses are common in our blood, skin, lungs, intestines, and oral/nasal cavity. Biologist Lynn Margulis describes the vital quality of viruses to human life succinctly (1998: 64): "We can no more be cured of our viruses than we can be relieved of our brain's frontal lobe; we are our viruses."

This discovery of nonpathogenic viruses opens the door for us to understand how viruses fit in God's good creation, and can be harnessed for greater good for humans and others. Some viruses are clearly beneficial to their host and even life-giving. We have known for a long time that viral infections at a young age are beneficial for strengthening our immune system to protect against infections later in life. But the explosion of data about viruses has revealed many more beneficial effects of viruses throughout the biosphere. Virologists often cite the example of the herpes virus in mice, which protects them against bacterial infections.

Professor Marilyn Roossinck is one of the leading researchers in the field, and she has discovered many beneficial functions of viruses. She has shown that pararetroviruses protect plants against pathogenic viruses (Roossinck 2005). Her research has demonstrated how four different viruses enabled several food crops (rice, tomato, squash, beets) to withstand severe drought conditions (Roossinck 2015). Her studies have revealed that viruses enable plants to survive in the extreme heat conditions of volcanic soil in Costa Rica and geothermal regions in Yellowstone National Park (Roossinck 2015).

Viruses play a beneficial role for humans too. We now know that eukaryotic viruses are as necessary to good intestinal health in humans as good bacteria (Liu 2019; Minton 2019). Carl Zimmer reports, "viruses help produce much of the oxygen we breathe and help control the planet's thermostat. ... Earth is a planet of viruses." (2015: 9). Thomas Pradeu of the University of Bordeaux has shown that retroviruses are necessary in the development of the placenta in mammals, including humans (Pradeu 2016). Good viruses will also protect against and fight off viral and non-viral diseases. This discovery is especially important in the fight against HIV and AIDS. A latent form of the herpes virus protects against some bacterial infections.

As our knowledge of viruses increases we are better able to harness the abilities of viruses to do good. Judy Diamond writes:

> Viruses are unseen but dynamic players in the ecology of Earth. They move DNA between species, provide new genetic material for evolution, and regulate vast populations of organisms. Every species, from tiny microbes to large animals, is influenced by the actions of viruses. Viruses extend their impact beyond species to affect climate, soil, the oceans, and fresh water. When you consider how every animal, plant and microbe has been shaped through the course of evolution, one has to consider the influential role played by the tiny and powerful viruses that share this planet. . . .
>
> But scientists also discovered new ways to harness the amazing diversity of viruses for our benefit.
>
> (cited from Zimmer 2015: ix-x).

The future of virus research includes the therapeutic benefits of viruses. Since the 1940s the standard treatment for bacterial infections in the Western world has been antibiotics. But antibiotics can also destroy good bacteria and cause intestinal and digestive problems. Furthermore, harmful bacteria can easily become resistant to antibiotics. Scientists now realize that antibiotics are not a good weapon against bacterial infections. Fortunately, they are also discovering that some viruses are very effective in killing bacteria. These could quickly replace the need for antibiotics. One group of viruses in particular have demonstrated their value in this matter, phages.

Phages were discovered in 1915 by Frederick Twort, an English Physician, and then again independently in 1917 by Felix d'Herelle, a Canadian doctor. Herelle named these viruses bacteriophages, that is "bacteria eaters" but today they are known simply as phages. It was not until the 1940s, with the invention of the electron microscope that scientists were able to confirm Herelle's discovery. Nevertheless Herelle had seen the potential of these phages to cure disease, so he did not wait for confirmation before using phages on his patients. Before giving phages to his patients, however, he tested their safety on himself, ingesting some and injecting others into his skin "without detecting the slightest malaise." Satisfied with his check, he began giving them to his patients. He gave them to WW1 soldiers suffering from dysentery, and they quickly recovered. Other patients were cured of cholera and the bubonic plague. Herelle soon became famous and in 1925 Sinclair Lewis wrote a best-selling novel, *Arrowsmith*, based on Herelle's work. In 1931 the book became a movie. Herelle later produced commercial preparations that were sold by the L'Oreal company. However, by the time the electron microscope confirmed Herelle's discoveries, Western medicine had become convinced of the safety and superiority of synthetic antibiotics to fight bacteria. The idea of injecting a live virus into a patient seemed irresponsible and dangerous. Remember, at that time a virus was defined as a disease causing agent. Consequently phage research and therapy dwindled to almost nothing in the West. In Central and Eastern Europe, however, particularly in the Soviet Union, phage research continued. Only in the last few decades, as problems mounted for antibiotics, has the West returned to consider the value of phage viruses.

Meanwhile, researchers have seen that viruses, by their very nature, are particularly adept at moving genes into host cells and then replicating those genes. Therefore, given this ability, scientists have asked, could viruses be used to carry healthy genes into diseased cells to promote healing (Warnock 2011)? If so, viruses could be used to treat cancer and other diseases. The potential for such treatment is great, since viruses are capable of transferring these therapeutic genes into parts of the body that are especially difficult for doctors to access, such as the brain. Similarly, Mario Mietzsch and Mavis Agbandjie-McKenna report that oncolytic viruses are now being studied for their ability to selectively destroy cancer cells without harming non-cancerous cells (Mietzsch 2017).

The Coronavirus

The coronavirus currently infecting humans is a novel strain. Therefore, we have no inherent defense against it, and we know very little about it. But we are learning much every day. Coronaviruses are a large family consisting of hundreds of various viruses. These inhabit animals, such as pigs, camels, bats, and cats without negative effects. However, some of these have circulated to human hosts. Seven of these coronaviruses are pathogenic in humans; four of those seven cause mild or moderate disease; three cause more severe and even fatal disease. These last three have occurred only in the last two decades. In November 2002 the SARS coronavirus (SARS-CoV) emerged, possibly originating in bats and circulating through civet cats before infecting humans. In September 2012 the MERS coronavirus was identified, possibly originating in camels. COVID-19 emerged in late 2019, probably originating in bats.

It is likely that bats were the original host of this virus and that they were not harmed in any way by the virus. It is also possible that the virus offered something beneficial to the bats. Researchers are looking into this question. Wynne and Wang (2013) have written, "Considering that bats are extremely long lived for their body size and that they demonstrate low rates of tumorigenesis, it is possible that some bat viruses may have oncolytic behavior. . . . It seems plausible that some of the viruses that bats harbor may have oncolytic properties that confer antitumor activity to the host."

Conclusion

How does the story of creation reframe the pandemic? This survey of research on viruses reveals that they are part of the good earth that God created and that humans are responsible to subdue, harness, and cultivate for the good of the world. Viruses are integral to the flourishing of life on the earth. We are just now discovering the remarkable abundance of viruses on the planet and how they function within particular environments. They enable life to thrive in great diversity around the globe. We are also learning how to harness their ability to transfer genes for additional benefits to humanity. We are also learning that disruptions to the environment stimulate the migration of viruses to different hosts, which presents the danger that they can become pathogenic. Disruptions to the planet are sometimes caused by human carelessness and sometimes by human recklessness in exploiting the environment for selfish and greedy gain. The sins of humanity have affected our environment and are undoubtedly related to the inexpedient outbursts of the natural realm. Carl Zimmer describes the task facing humanity (Roossinck 2016: 6):

> Learning about the diversity of viruses is not just a fascinating experience but a vital one. We need to understand where the next deadly pandemic will emerge from and what its vulnerabilities are. As scientists discover new kinds of viruses, they're also converting some of them into tools, to control bacteria, deliver genes, and even build nanomaterials. By appreciating the beauty of viruses, we can better understand nature's inventiveness, even as we learn lessons about how to avoid becoming its victims.

Since, within the Genesis narrative, humanity has been given responsibility to govern and steward the natural world, it can be said that humans are at least indirectly responsible for the migration of the coronavirus to human hosts. Perhaps the most likely scenario is that the migration and shift to pathogenic status was not caused by specifically identifiable steps as much as it was the consequence of the disruption in the natural order caused by a myriad of abuses over a long period of time. We might say, then, that the emergence of a pathogenic coronavirus is the expected consequence of a natural order subjected to careless governors. The current outbreak may be heard as the created realm's groanings in bondage to corruption. The Apostle Paul describes the situation in Romans 8.19-22:

> For the creation waits with eager longing for the revealing of the sons of God. For the creation was subjected to futility, not willingly, but because of him who subjected it,

in hope that the creation itself will be set free from its bondage to corruption and obtain the freedom of the glory of the children of God. For we know that the whole creation has been groaning together in the pains of childbirth until now.

3

OMEGA
Creation Flourishing

Introduction

The end of the Christian story reveals the triumph of God's original design and intention for His creation. In our final vision of heaven and earth in Revelation 21-22 we see the world flourishing under the faithful stewardship of humanity. God has overcome humanity's rebellion and restored them to their rightful position stewarding his creation. They now cultivate and care for the creation faithfully. In the book of Revelation John describes the end in such a way as to tie the end to the beginning, so that the end reveals the success of God's plans announced at the beginning. One way to summarize this idea is in the oft-cited phrase, "The End is in the Beginning." But we will discover that while the end was there in the beginning in potential, the end has some surprises to reveal as well. The goodness implanted by God in the creation, when cultivated faithfully, reveals a brilliance and beauty far beyond the capacity of language to describe, so that John was forced to pile symbol upon symbol in trying to convey the reality.

The End is in the Beginning

The early Christians conceived of the end of this present world in terms and concepts derived from the beginning of the world. The Epistle of Barnabas, written c. 130 CE, is often cited as an example: "The Lord says, 'Behold, I will make the last things like the first'" (*Epistle of Barnabas* 6.13). Early Christian historiography was undeniably progressive and forward-looking, but when it reached its goal, that goal appeared much like the original garden restored. The life, death, resurrection, and ascension of Jesus excited his followers to believe that God was renewing His work in the world. They believed that Jesus had inaugurated God's kingdom and that the end-times had invaded the present. God's ultimate plan for the world had received a definitive breakthrough with the death and resurrection of Jesus. But what was that plan? What was God's intention for the world? What would the end look like? These questions led the early Christians back to Genesis 1-2 to understand God's original design for the world. Trusting that God would ultimately achieve his plans for the world, the early Christians shaped their vision of the future around those images from the beginning. That climactic vision is brilliantly described in John's Apocalypse, and it serves as the capstone of the grand narrative.

We find the origins of this practice of looking backward to understand the future in the teachings of Jesus himself. "As it was in the days of Noah, so it will be at the coming of the Son of Man" (Matthew 24.47). Jesus read the Law and Prophets as signs and types pointing forward to himself (Luke 24.27). This practice inspired his followers to re-examine all those ancient texts in that new light (Matthew 2.5-6, 15, 17, 23, etc.). The result of this re-examination was a uniquely Christian re-telling of the biblical story, whereby Jesus not only inaugurated the fulfillment of the biblical hope for God's kingdom, but did so by launching a reiteration of the biblical story, beginning with Genesis and the Adam story. Within the Old Testament Adam, Eve and Eden had virtually disappeared after Genesis 5. Other sects within Judaism thought of the end in terms of the beginning, but none developed the idea as vigorously and fully as the early Christians. For example, a fragmentary text from the Dead Sea Scrolls reads "and all the world will be like Eden" (4Q475; cf. 4Q428 5). And Psalms of Solomon 14.2-3 says "His pious ones are the paradise of the Lord, the trees of life; their planting is rooted forever; they shall not be plucked up all the days of heaven." It was the earliest followers of Jesus who revived these stories and found in them analogies of the coming kingdom of God and a new humanity. The next generation of Christian writers developed this theme further.

The Apostle Paul's contributions in developing this theme are particularly important. Paul saw Jesus as a second Adam, inaugurating a new humanity that would fulfill God's original intention for all humanity. He described Adam as a "type of the one to come" (Romans 5.14). He unfolds the importance of this idea in his letter to the Corinthians:

> The first Adam became a living being; the last Adam became a life-giving spirit. . . . The first man was from the earth, a man of dust; the second man is from heaven. As was the man of dust, so also are those who are of dust, and

as is the man of heaven, so also are those of heaven. Just as
we have borne the image of the man of dust, we shall also
bear the image of the man of heaven.
(1 Corinthians 15.45-49)

The End is in the Future—But Penetrates the Present

This return-to-the-garden motif proved to be fruitful and flexible
in early Christian literature. It could be used to describe the future
paradise beyond the present world, but it could also be used to
describe a present reality of believers, due to their spiritual union
with Jesus through the Holy Spirit. The first usage of the garden
motif—to describe the future world—is illustrated in a story told in
The Martyrdom of Saints Perpetua and Felicity, written c. 209 CE
(Heffernan 2012: 62). The second usage—to describe a present
reality through spiritual union with Christ—is found a generation
earlier (c. 160 CE) in the anonymous Epistle to Diognetus. We will
consider both briefly, before looking at John's vision. They prepare
us to recognize and understand the fullness of John's description
of the garden in Revelation 21-22 as the summation of the
Christian Story.

The Garden is Future

Perpetua and Felicity were martyred with other Christians at a civic
celebration in Carthage, North Africa, on the birthday of the
Emperor Septimus Severus in March 203. Just prior to her
martyrdom, while in prison awaiting execution, Perpetua had a
vision in which she ascends a tall and narrow bronze ladder into

heaven. She explains that at the foot of the ladder there was "a serpent lying, marvelously great, which lay in wait for those that would go up, and frightened them that they might not go up." She then sees Saturus, who was the first in the group to be martyred, near the top of the ladder, who turns and says to her, "Perpetua, I await you, but see that the serpent bite you not." Perpetua responds, "It shall not hurt me—in the name of Jesus Christ." Perpetua then steps on the head of the snake and begins her ascent. Along the way, attached to the sides of the ladder, she sees instruments of torture: swords, lances, hooks, knives, and daggers. And upon her arrival at the top, she reports her view, "I saw a very great space of garden, and in the midst a man sitting, white-headed, in shepherd's clothing, tall, milking his sheep. Standing around in white were many thousands. He raised his head and looked at me, and said, 'Welcome, child.'"

This is a remarkable piece of literature, describing Perpetua's ascent into the heavenly realm, employing striking allusions to Genesis. The ladder imagery alludes to Jacob's ladder reaching from earth to heaven and serving as the gate of heaven (Genesis 28.10-17). The serpent image is a direct reference to Genesis 3, where God curses the serpent, saying, "I will put hatred between you and the woman, and between your offspring and her offspring. He will crush your head, and you will bite his heel" (3.15). Perpetua steps on the serpent, joining with many other faithful Christians in the fulfillment of that text (cf. Romans 16.20). But most clearly, when she arrives in heaven, she finds that heaven is an expansive garden, where the good shepherd is feeding his sheep. The ancient garden is the future home of the faithful ones. The end is a return to the beginning.

**The Garden is Present**

Several decades earlier (c. 160 CE), the Epistle to Diognetus, "widely recognized as one of the true literary gems of early Christianity" (Ehrman 2003: 122), illustrates another way the garden motif provided guidance for Christians. In a somewhat confusing metaphor, the faithful followers of Jesus (the second Adam) become the present iteration of the garden and its trees, and are nurtured to bear fruit by the indwelling Word. The Psalms of Solomon 14.2-3, written 200 years earlier, had said "His pious ones are the paradise of the Lord, the trees of life; their planting is rooted forever; they shall not be plucked up all the days of heaven." The unknown author of the Epistle adopts this image of the pious as the garden and applies it more vigorously to the followers of Jesus, the Word, which dwells in them. These faithful ones are cultivated and bear fruit through their knowledge of the Word dwelling in them (12.1-2a):

> When you read these things and hear them eagerly, you will know what God provides for those who love properly, you who have become a paradise of delight, who have made a fertile and fruitful tree spring up in yourselves, you who are laden with various kinds of fruit. For in this place were planted a Tree of Knowledge and a Tree of Life.

The author quickly explains that the presence of the Tree of Knowledge is not a danger for followers of Jesus, but an opportunity. "It is not the Tree of Knowledge that kills; rather, it is disobedience" (12.2b). He says that the Tree was meant for good, but it was used wrongly (12.3-5):

In the beginning God planted a Tree of Knowledge and a Tree of Life in the middle of the paradise, thereby revealing life through knowledge. But those who were there at the beginning made use of it in an impure way, and became naked through the deceit of the serpent. For life cannot exist without knowledge nor secure knowledge apart from life. For this reason each was planted next to the other. When the Apostle considered this marvel he criticized knowledge that is exercised apart from the true command that leads to life, saying, "knowledge puffs up, but love builds up."

Therefore, the author encourages Diognetus that true knowledge—knowledge of Jesus Christ—leads to life. Diognetus should cultivate this tree and eat its fruit (12.6-8):

The one who has come to know with reverential fear, and who seeks life, plants in hope and expects to receive fruit. Let your heart be knowledge and your life be true, comprehensible Word. If you bear this tree and pluck its fruit, you will always harvest what God desires. The serpent cannot touch such things nor can deceit defile them.

For the author of this letter, the garden God intended from the beginning has now been restored metaphorically in Jesus and his followers, and is being cultivated as Jesus the Word lives through his people. The passage is reminiscent of Jesus' teaching "I am the vine and you are the branches. If you remain in me and I in you,

you will bear much fruit" (John 15.5), but the primary images are drawn from Genesis. This present-time realization of the garden reality stands in contrast to Perpetua's vision of the garden as a future destination in the afterlife. However, both of these ideas are united in the most important garden text in the New Testament, Revelation 21-22.

The End in Revelation 21-22—Garden-City-Sanctuary-People

John's vision in Revelation 21-22 provides the canonical summation to the Christian grand narrative. While it very clearly draws on the garden imagery of Genesis, it also develops that imagery, revealing that the garden has been undergoing faithful cultivation for many generations, since at least the time of Christ, and all that work will be displayed in all its glory in the unspecified future. It is much more than the garden of Eden. The progressive expansion of the garden is seen in its massive size; the faithful cultivation of the garden's resources is seen in its new manifestation as a city; and the fulfillment of the garden's purpose is realized as it becomes the home of God and humanity together.

There is no doubt that John intended his readers to understand his final vision as the restored Garden of Eden, since he identifies the Tree of Life growing on both sides of the River of the Water of Life (Revelation 22.1-2). But the garden imagery quickly recedes into the background and a new image becomes central and controlling: the city. The garden is now set within a city. John says the river flows "through the middle of the street of the city" (22.2). An angel has a measuring rod and tells John the size and shape of the city (21.15-17), and describes its walls and gates (21.10-14,

17-21). Its size is impossibly immense, covering the entirety of the earth, indicating it is symbolic of the whole of creation, and its shape is a perfect cube, like the holy of holies where God dwelt.

The significance of the transformation of the garden into a city is that the city is often regarded as humanity's greatest cultural achievement. God did not create a city in the beginning; He gave humanity that task. Cities are the natural outgrowth of humanity's inherent design; made in the image of God, they express their creativity, intelligence, and desire for relationship by building cities where their gifts can flourish in cooperation with each other. Aristotle famously said "a human is by nature a political animal"—that is made for a *polis*, a city—"and that anyone without a city . . . is either a wild beast or a god" (Politics 1.2-3). To construct and maintain a city requires that humans exert their God-given gifts to the greatest extent and in the greatest cooperation.

John says the city was built of pure gold, clear as glass (21.18), but he focuses on the construction of the walls and gates of the city, describing them as made from twelve different precious stones (jasper, sapphire, agate, emerald, etc.; 21.19-20) and huge pearls. "Each gate was made of a single pearl" (21.21). There are two possible reasons for John's fixation on precious stones and pearls. The first is that they are natural resources; the second is their association with Rome.

First, then, precious stones and pearls are not man-made. They are products of the earth. They are natural resources. We see, then, that humanity's greatest work, the city, is achieved by making use of nature's resources in creative ways. The garden of the earth produces the materials for humanity to build their cities. This is a picture of humanity fulfilling its vocation as God's stewards, subduing the powers of the earth and cultivating its products.

Second, precious stones and pearls were regarded by Romans as a particularly splendid work of nature. Pliny the Elder writes about them at great length in *Natural History* book 37. He introduces his discussion, saying (37.1.1):

> It remains for me to speak of precious stones: a subject in which the majestic might of Nature presents itself to us, contracted within a very limited space, though, in the opinion of many, nowhere displayed in a more admirable form. So great is the value that men attach to the multiplied varieties of these gems, their numerous colors, their constituent parts, and their singular beauty, that, in the case of some of them, it is looked upon as no less than sacrilege to engrave them, for signets even, the very purpose for which, in reality, they were made. Others, again, are regarded as beyond all price, and could not be valued at any known amount by human wealth; so much so that, in the case of many, it is quite sufficient to have some single gem or other before the eyes, there to behold the supreme and absolute perfection of Nature's work.

Precious stones and pearls were a special feature of Pompey's display in his triumphal procession after the Third Mithridatic War (74-62 BCE). Pliny the Elder writes, "it was this conquest by Pompey the Great that first introduced so general a taste for pearls and precious stones." (37.6.1). Pliny then quotes from the public register (37.6.2):

> [Pompey the Great] displayed in public a chess board with its pieces made of two precious stones three feet in width

by two in length—and to leave no doubt that the resources of Nature do become exhausted, I will observe, that no precious stones are to be found at the present day, at all approaching such dimensions as these; as also that there was upon this board a moon of solid gold, thirty pounds in weight!—three banqueting couches, vessels for nine waiters, in gold and precious stones; three golden statues of Minerva, Mars, and Apollo; thirty-three crowns adorned with pearls; a square mountain of gold, with stags upon it, lions, and all kinds of fruit, and surrounded with a vine of gold; as also a museum, adorned with pearls, with an horologe upon the top of it.

Pliny also describes (37.6.2):

a likeness in pearls of Pompey himself!—his noble countenance, with the hair thrown back from the forehead, delighting the eye. Yes, I say, those frank features, so venerated throughout all nations, were here displayed in pearls! . . . Thy portrait in pearls, O Great One! Those resources of prodigality that have been discovered for the sake of females only! Thy portrait in pearls, refinements in luxury, which the Roman laws would not have allowed thee to wear even! Was it in this way that thy value must be appreciated?

Rome's appreciation for pearls and precious stones provides a contrasting parallel with John's city.

John's city, the New Jerusalem, is described as a holy city (21.2, 10). It is placed in striking contrast to the evil city named "Babylon the Great" (18.2), the archetype of humanity's cultivation of a city contrary to God's plans. The whole world marveled at Babylon the Great because of its wealth and power. But it had achieved its greatness by wielding its powers ruthlessly and by exploiting others for its own selfish pleasure (Revelation 18). It is clear that John's "Babylon the Great" is modeled on Rome, because it was the current manifestation of humanity's violent, exploitative, and oppressive dominion. John's good news is that "Babylon has fallen!" (18.2) and that the New Jerusalem is eternal (22.5).

Adamic Humanity's efforts to subdue the earth and cultivate its resources (precious stones and pearls), creating a great city (Babylon or Rome), come crashing down to ruin. The city was built on an alternative vision of reality that claimed greatness can be achieved by exploitation, oppression and injustice, wholly contrary to God's design in creation. Because of the innate design of nature, cultivation that runs contrary to that design cannot prevail and will ultimately collapse. Only work done in harmony with the design of nature will ultimately stand. John's vision of the end, therefore, reveals that God's plan for humanity to steward the earth toward something beautiful will ultimately be achieved, but only when humanity pursues that work in accordance with God's will and design. The precious stones and pearls belong to the New Jerusalem, not to Babylon.

John further describes the city as made of pure gold and in the shape of a perfect cube (21.16). This can only be symbolic; and its literary allusion clarifies what it symbolizes. John alludes to 1 Kings 6 where the construction of Solomon's Temple is described. The inner sanctuary, the holy of holies, wherein dwelt the glorious presence of God, is described as "overlaid with pure gold" and shaped as a perfect cube, "its length, width and height all the same"

(1 Kings 6.20). For John, then, the entire city, which embraces the whole of creation, has become God's sanctuary, his dwelling place. This is the crowning achievement of God and humanity working together—Creator and steward crafting a home where they live together. The garden-city is actually a garden-city-sanctuary. John writes:

> Then I saw a new heaven and a new earth, for the first heaven and the first earth had passed away, and the sea was no more. And I saw the holy city, new Jerusalem, coming down out of heaven from God, prepared as a bride adorned for her husband. And I heard a loud voice from the throne saying, "Behold, the dwelling place of God is with humanity. He will dwell with them, and they will be his people. God himself will be with them as their God." (Revelation 21.1-3)

But there is one final feature of John's vision of the garden-city-sanctuary. We have pointed out throughout this discussion that the whole vision is symbolic. The descriptions of the size and shape of the city are physically impossible, but as symbols they are meaningful. Scholars have pointed out that the garden-city-sanctuary is a symbol of the people of God who make up the city; that is, the city is not as much place as it is people. The city is people. An angel explains to John, "Come, I will show you the Bride, the wife of the Lamb. And he carried me away in the Spirit to a great high mountain, and showed me the holy city Jerusalem" (21.9-10). The holy city is the bride of Christ, the people of God. This last feature is found in the Apostle Paul's teachings too, for he envisioned the people of God as the new temple of God, the place where God dwelt. "Do you not know that you are God's Temple, and God's Spirit dwells in you?" (1 Corinthians 3.16; cf. 6.19). 1 Peter 2.4-5 makes the same point:

> As you come to him [Jesus Christ], a living stone rejected by men, but in the sight of God chosen and precious, you yourselves like living stones are being built up as a spiritual house, to be a holy priesthood, to offer spiritual sacrifices to God through Jesus Christ.

For John, then, the garden-city-sanctuary-people is both the future goal of humanity and its present project. We are in the process of becoming what God originally designed us to be. We are the sanctuary in progress. Perpetua's vision is in harmony with John: we are climbing the ladder that leads to the heavenly garden; but the disciple who wrote to Diognetus was also faithful to John's vision when he pictured the garden as the people of God being cultivated in the present. For John the end is in the beginning, but it is much more than the beginning image revealed. It is the realization of the hope that the beginning offered; it is the full flowering of the original potencies. The end is in the beginning, as the tree is in the seed.

Conclusion

John brings the grand narrative to its climax, and reveals that its glorious end is currently in progress. The goodness of the original creation has prevailed. The original garden was pregnant with potential, but needed humanity's nurturing hand to guide it toward birth. The new garden-city-sanctuary-people is flourishing with life and bears the marks of human creativity, design and cultivation. The original garden was small and needed to be extended and populated—"be fruitful and multiply and fill the earth and subdue it" (Genesis 1.28). The new garden-city-sanctuary-people extends throughout the world and is populated by every nation, people group, and language group (Revelation 5.9; 7.9; 11.9). "The nations are guided by its light and the kings of the earth bring their glory into it" (21.24). The original garden was home to both God and humans briefly, but humans were banished from the garden and prevented from returning (Genesis 3.23-24). The new garden is the permanent home for God and humanity. "Behold, the tabernacling of God is with humanity. He will live with them, and they will be his people, and God himself will be with them as their God." (Revelation 21.3). All the stains of humanity's evil and corruption have been cleansed and washed away; the curse of pain, disease, and death have been removed. "He will wipe away every tear from their eyes, and death will be no more, neither will there be mourning nor crying nor pain, for the former things have passed away." (21.4). "No longer will there be any curse" (22.3). "The leaves of the tree of life are for the healing of the nations" (22.2). The whole creation is now functioning as it was divinely designed and originally intended. God is reigning over His creation, with humanity at his side, in the place of honor, exercising obedient stewardship over the earth. "God will be their light and they will reign forever and ever" (22.5). The creation is as it was always meant to be.

PART II

Bridging Alpha & Omega

CONSPECTUS OF PART II

In Part I, "Alpha & Omega", we saw that God created a good world, with dynamic potential to display his glorious gifts. We saw that humanity was charged with the responsibility to guide its potential toward that end. Tragically, however, we also saw that humanity fell short in their vocation and initiated a march toward destruction and death for all living things. The coronavirus pandemic is one iteration of that long death march. Happily, we saw that the end of the story reveals not destruction and death but the realization of God's original design and intention. This leaves us with questions. How was the predicament rectified? What path must the story take in order to arrive at this conclusion? Can these two window panes be linked? A further difficulty emerges when we consider that the opening and closing frames are idealistic, and utopian. They are not reports of concrete historical events, but visions of another world. How do those visionary worlds relate to our real world? Is this optimistic reframing just a dream of utopian visionaries?

Part II, "Bridging Alpha & Omega", answers these questions. The central pane, through which we look at the coronavirus in Part II, is not visionary; it is historical. The events it describes occur on the ground in the real world. The pane we look through is the life of Jesus of Nazareth. The accomplishments of Jesus provide a bridge from Genesis to Revelation, from blueprint to completed construction. The visionary worlds of the original creation and the new creation are linked in the life of Jesus. The visionary world inspires and clarifies his mission in the real world. He has come to rescue the real world from certain destruction and death and to bring into realization the glorious world previously seen only in vision.

In chapter 4, "Jesus' World: Creation Broken and Deadly", we find Jesus firmly embedded within the world we know well, a world of death and disease, a world heading for disaster, destruction, and death. Jesus understood well the world's condition and need for rescue. Historians and other scholars tell us that health conditions in the first century, particularly in ancient Judea, were far worse than we experience today. Thus, Jesus' response to disease and illness in his day reveal much about how his followers should respond to the coronavirus pandemic today. In chapter 5, "Jesus Heals: Rescue Signaled", we learn that Jesus' healing ministry was not an end in itself, but a pointer toward a deeper and more significant healing. These healings reveal Jesus' identity and mission. He is the Son of Man who has come to inaugurate the kingdom of God and thereby rescue the world from destruction and death. In chapter 6, "Jesus Dies & Rises: Rescue Effected", we dive deeper into the identity of Jesus as Son of Man and his mission to inaugurate the kingdom of God. We learn that as Son of Man Jesus identifies with humanity and accomplishes humanity's vocation. We learn, too, that it is through his death, resurrection, and ascension that Jesus accomplishes his mission to rescue humanity from certain destruction and to reestablish humanity as rulers over God's creation. His accomplishments provide confidence that he has initiated and effected a rescue operation that will ultimately bring about the garden-city-sanctuary-people vision of Revelation 21-22. In chapter 7, "Jesus' Followers: Rescue Progresses", we consider briefly the progress that has been made toward the full realization of that vision.

4

JESUS' WORLD
Creation Broken and Deadly

Introduction

It is common for people to have romantic and idealized images of Jesus in his world, walking the green hills of Galilee and the sandy shores by the lake. But these images are completely mistaken. The world of Jesus is well-known to historians and it was a world that none of us would want to live in. Poor hygiene and sanitation meant gastrointestinal diseases were common. And the lack of health care meant that people suffered from chronic diseases until death. Few people lived beyond 30 years. Jesus knew very well that the world he lived in was broken and deadly. This brief chapter paints a picture of that world.

Infectious and Parasitic Disease in Jesus' World

The coronavirus may not have been present when Jesus walked the hills and shores of Galilee and the streets of Jerusalem, but he was no stranger to comparable infectious diseases and other serious illnesses. Jesus was both a Teacher and a Healer. He healed those who were blind, deaf, lame, crippled, deformed, feverish, bleeding, as well as those with unspecified mysterious illnesses. Infectious and parasitic diseases were common in his environment. Indeed, Jesus would have been confronted with debilitating diseases far more often than we are today. Jonathan Reed writes,

> Life in first-century Galilee . . . was substantially different from the modern world and cannot be characterized as stable. Chronic and seasonal disease, especially malaria, cut down significant segments of the population and left even the healthy quite often ill. . . . The evidence for low life expectancy in antiquity, albeit circumstantial, is abundant.
> (Reed 2014: 242)

The hot summer months were particularly devastating and deaths spiked every year from August to October. Reed states,

> The seasonal rhythm of death indicates that Mediterranean populations suffered from a plethora of quick-killing gastrointestinal and respiratory diseases such as dysentery, typhus, typhoid, tuberculosis, plague, and especially malaria. . . . Hot weather made contagious malarial fevers acute and agitated gastrointestinal diseases.
> (Reed 2010: 355)

Archaeologists working throughout Israel, including Jerusalem and Galilee, have discovered many first century sites that reveal much about the morbidity and mortality of Jesus' contemporaries.

Many and varied intestinal parasites have been found in archaeological sites in the Dead Sea region, including roundworm, whipworm, pinworm, and others (Mitchell 2016: 595). Half of the combs found in archaeological sites around the Dead Sea (Masada, Qumran, the Negev) are infested with lice and lice eggs (Mumcuouglu 2003). The area around the Sea of Galilee was breeding ground for the mosquito (*anopheles*) carrying malaria. Reed (2010, 357) states, "Evidence from antiquity confirms that malaria was a problem in and around Galilee." He cites, for example, Josephus, the first century Jewish historian from Galilee, who describes the areas south of the lake as "pestilent and disease ridden" (*Wars of the Jews*, 4.456). The first century Galilean Rabbi Hanina ben Dosa was famous for his prayers for the sick; it is said that his prayers healed Gamaliel's son of the fever (b.Ber. 34b). Luke, the physician, describes the healing of Peter's mother-in-law and diagnoses her as being "overwhelmed by a great fever" (Luke 4.38). The ancient malady described as a "great fever" is now commonly believed to be malaria. Archaeologists have found in the Galilean regions where Jesus walked magical amulets designed to ward off "the great fever". Dr. Israel Kligler, a medical historian at the Hebrew University of Jerusalem in the 1920s, wrote a massive study titled *The Epidemiology and Control of Malaria in Palestine* (1930), in which he described the region of the Lower Galilee where Jesus grew up as "one of the most malarious in Palestine" (p. 41).

In addition to malaria, Israelites also suffered from tuberculosis and Hansen's disease. Advances in genetics enable archaeologists to analyze DNA from skeletal remains found in tombs. More than 70 family tombs have been found in the Lower Hinnom Valley at the foot of Mount Zion in Jerusalem (the area known as Akeldama, the field of blood: Matthew 27.3-8; Acts 1.19). One of these first century tombs was a family tomb containing several generations, known as the Tomb of the Shroud because a shroud was found in it. DNA analysis of several bone fragments revealed two pathogens: *Mycobacterium tuberculosis* and *Mycobacterium leprae*, indicating the presence of tuberculosis and leprosy—Hansen's disease (Mathewson 2009). This is the earliest known case of Hansen's disease in Israel. These diseases caused serious deformities, sometimes causing their victims to become crippled and lame. Debilitated persons were typically shunned by society. Jesus often encountered these people.

Archaeologists working in the ancient village of Meiron in the Upper Galilee, uncovered a complex of tombs in which villagers were buried over a span of four centuries. 197 individuals were identified and their bones analyzed.

> The analysis of the skeletal remains proved to be especially illuminating and significant. First, the population in the Meiron tomb over the four centuries of its use resembles the population of Jerusalem and Ein Gedi in the same period in terms of stature. Second, infant and child mortality was high—c. 50%—because of endemic disease among other factors.
> (Meyer and Meyers 2015: 382-83)

Excavations in the foothills of Judea, the Shephelah, revealed a complex of tombs in which 227 individuals were identified. Skeletal analysis revealed the average life-span to be about 24 years. (Reed 2010: 354). Similar results were uncovered in the south of Judea, the Negev, where the remains of at least 289 individuals were studied (Nagar 2008). Yossi Nagar reports that "the populations suffered a relatively high frequency of infectious diseases, to which it had low durability" (Nagar 2008: 89). He calculates that life expectancy at birth was 26 years, but if one lived to be 10 years old, then life expectancy was 30 years. Nagar adds that these numbers are "slightly higher" than the life expectancy numbers for Castra [Haifa], which was 24-25 years if one reached age 10, and Beth Shean, which was 29 years.

These studies illumine the world of Jesus and explain his fame as a healer. Given the severe infant mortality rate it is hardly surprising that mothers brought their babies to Jesus to be blessed by him (Mark 10.13; Luke 18.15-17). Neither is it surprising that Joseph, Jesus' father, is nowhere on the scene. From the earliest period it was simply assumed, and reasonably so, that he had died. And of course it is not surprising that crowds of people suffering from various crippling diseases flocked around Jesus when he demonstrated his ability to heal.

Conclusion

Idealized pastoral images of Jesus walking the green hills of Galilee are simply not accurate. The world of Jesus was marked by disease and death. Richard Rohrbaugh (1996: 5) sums up the quality of life and health at that time:

> Studies by paleopathologists indicate that infectious disease and malnutrition were widespread. By age thirty the majority suffered from internal parasites, their teeth were rotted, their eyesight gone. Most had lived with the debilitating results of protein deficiency since

childhood. . . . Given poor housing, non-existent sanitation, economically inaccessible medical care, and bad diet—one fourth of a Palestinian peasant's 1,800 calories per day came from alcohol—one begins to revise the romanticized picture many twentieth century Americans have of Jesus' audience.

Jesus came to a world desperately broken. He came to heal and restore. The next chapter reveals the significance of his healing ministry.

5

JESUS HEALS
Rescue Signaled

Introduction

Jesus' initial response to a world marked by disease and death was to heal it. He had compassion on the sick and suffering. He cared for them, and in so doing he revealed God's care for them. Jesus healed people suffering from many different illnesses and maladies. Similarly, he also demonstrated his authority to subdue the dangerous and destructive powers of the natural world that threatened human health and life, such as storms on the sea of Galilee. This chapter offers a brief survey of these two dramatic aspects of Jesus' ministry and their significance, healing human bodies and restraining nature's threats. These actions are often called miracles, but they are more accurately regarded as signs. They were not an end in themselves; instead, they pointed to something greater, bigger, deeper—they signaled that God had resumed his work to reclaim, redeem, and restore his creation through Jesus. They signaled Jesus' true identity and his larger mission.

Jesus as Healer of Disease: Signs of Something Greater

It is clear that disease and healing were a major concern of Jesus. John Meier (1990: 1321) has said, "Nothing is more certain about Jesus than that he was viewed by his contemporaries as an exorcist and a healer." Stevan Davies agrees, describing it as "bedrock fact." He writes (Davies 2014: 197): "No fact about Jesus of Nazareth is so widely and repeatedly attested in the New Testament gospels as the fact that he was a healer of people in mental and physical distress." Jesus identified himself as a physician when he said, "Surely you will quote the proverb to me: 'Physician, heal yourself!' (Luke 4.23). And he explained his unusual behavior with the response, "It is not the healthy who need a physician but the sick" (Mark 2.17). The Gospels record a multitude of different types of healings: paralysis (Mark 2.1-12), curvature of the spine (Luke 13.10-17), excessive bleeding (Mark 5.24-34), blindness (Mark 8.22-26), deafness (Mark 7.31-37), and leprosy (i.e., skin eruptions; Mark 1.40-45), among others.

Jesus' healings were accomplished in public and were undeniable. Even those who opposed him believed he healed many people. They only questioned the source of his power, suggesting it was demonic (Luke 11.14-16). For Jesus, his healing power came from God and signaled the fact that God was once again actively pursuing his plans to rescue and restore the world (Matthew 12.22-28). More important than each individual healing, then, was the more expansive goal toward which these healings pointed. Jesus was on a mission to rescue God's world, to establish God's kingdom, and each person healed was a small sign that that larger work was now advancing.

The healings were not, therefore, the end or goal of Jesus' ministry; they were instead signals that God was at work doing something even greater. They were meant to point beyond the obvious and observable to the invisible spiritual realm. They were meant to reveal and authenticate the identity and mission of Jesus. Jesus was the Son of Man sent to inaugurate the kingdom of God.

Jesus' Healings Signal
His Mission to Inaugurate the Kingdom of God

The Gospel writers firmly connect Jesus' healing ministry with his announcement of the kingdom of God. Matthew introduces and summarizes the twofold ministry of Jesus—proclaiming the kingdom and healing every disease:

> Jesus went throughout Galilee, teaching in their synagogues, proclaiming the good news of the kingdom, and healing every disease and sickness among the people. News about him spread all over Syria, and people brought to him all who were ill with various diseases, those suffering severe pain, the demon possessed, those suffering seizures, and the paralyzed. And he healed them. (Matthew 4.23-24; cf. 9.35; 13.53-56)

His ability to heal the sick drew large crowds who listened to his teaching and proclamation of the kingdom.

> A large crowd of his disciples was there and a great number of people from all over Judea, from Jerusalem,

and from the coastal region around Tyre and Sidon, who had come to hear him and to be healed of their diseases. Those troubled by impure spirits were cured, and the people all tried to touch him, because power was coming from him and healing them all.
(Luke 6.17-19)

Jesus explained to his opposition, "If it is by the Spirit of God that I drive out demons, then the kingdom of God has come upon you" (Matthew 12.28).

Jesus' Healings Signal
His Identity as the Son of Man

Jesus' healing also revealed his identity as the Son of Man. Matthew explains that his healing of a paralyzed man was meant to demonstrate his identity and authority as the Son of Man who forgives sins. Matthew writes:

Jesus stepped into a boat, crossed over and came to his own town. Some men brought to him a paralyzed man, lying on a mat. When Jesus saw their faith, he said to the man, "Take heart, son, your sins are forgiven." At this, some of the teachers of the law said to themselves, "This fellow is blaspheming!" Knowing their thoughts, Jesus said, "Why do you entertain evil thoughts in your hearts? Which is easier: to say, 'Your sins are forgiven,' or to say, 'Get up and walk'? But I want you to know that the Son of Man has authority on earth to forgive sins." So he then

said to the paralyzed man, "Get up, take your mat and go home." Then the man got up and went home. When the crowd saw this, they were filled with awe, and they praised God, who had given such authority to man.
(Matthew 9.1-8)

In this encounter physical healing is meant to signal the deeper reality of spiritual healing, which likewise reveals the greater reality of Jesus' identity as the Son of Man with authority to forgive sins. Again we see that Jesus' healing ministry was not meant merely to heal the sick. It had the greater and deeper and more important goal of signaling that the Son of Man had arrived to inaugurate the kingdom of God, a world where disease does not exist and where health and fullness of life prevail. The kingdom is heralded by the restoration of humanity, physically, spiritually, and socially. He has come to restore proper order to the cosmos, reconciling God and humans, restructuring society, and healing broken bodies. He announced all of this in the synagogue in Nazareth:

> The Spirit of the Lord is upon me,
> Because He has anointed me
> To proclaim good news to the poor.
> He has sent me to proclaim freedom for the prisoners
> And recovery of sight to the blind,
> To set the oppressed free,
> To proclaim the year of the Lord's favor.
> (Luke 4.18)

We will consider this text more thoroughly in the next chapter.

Jesus' healing ministry was linked to his miracles in the natural world too, particularly involving the sea. Just as the human body needs healing and restoration, so too does the natural world. These miracles also reveal Jesus, as the Son of Man, asserting proper dominion over the creation as God's faithful steward. Jesus' authority over the natural world is demonstrated by calming storms at sea (Mark 4.35-41) and walking on the sea (Mark 6.45-52). These symbolic acts allude to the potential of the sea to overwhelm and to destroy. The stormy sea was a symbol of the threat to overturn the cosmic order with chaos (Genesis 1.2; Genesis 6-7; cf. Psalm 107.23-32). These stormy seas are not evil, but they are dangerous and must be controlled. They have the potential to harm, but also the potential for good. Jesus harnessed their powers for good, for example, when he sent Peter out into the deep waters, where Peter had a miraculous catch of fish (Luke 5.1-11). But the darker side of the sea is hinted at, for example, when we are told that our sins are cast far away into the sea (Micah 7.19), and that in the new creation there will be no more sea (Revelation 21.1).

More importantly, however, their potential for harm is illustrated by the monstrous beasts that rise up out of the stormy sea to exercise dominion over world empires (Daniel 7.3; cf. Revelation 13.1). The close connections made between the chaotic seas and the sinful rule of beastly kings indicate that the stormy seas are symbols of the chaos of the world under the sinful exercise of human dominion. Jesus' actions in subduing the sea and its threatening powers intimate his identity as the Danielic Son of

Man overcoming the dominion of the beasts rising out of the sea, and establishing the eternal kingdom of God (Daniel 7).

Again we see that Jesus' powerful acts are meant to point beyond the immediate circumstance to his greater work in rescuing the world from its corruption and impending destruction and death. The chaos of the seas is symbolic of the chaos in the world that needs to be subdued and stewarded. Sidney Greidanus identifies the various eruptions of chaos in our world that need to be subdued (2018: 9):

> Today we see this evil chaos east of Eden in the human race in the enmity between people, races, religions, and nation-states: wars, slavery, religious persecution, racism. We see this chaos in the swollen bellies of malnourished children; in people dying from cancer, Ebola, and other diseases and disasters; in the thousands of refugees fleeing their home countries, hundreds of them drowning as they cross dangerous seas in flimsy boats. We see this chaos in the violence perpetrated by drug cartels, in the senseless murders in our inner cities, in the rape of women and children, and in the spread of terror organizations whose goal is to destroy people, nations, and cultural treasures. . . . The implication is that Scripture views our struggles with pain, disease, disasters, and death in this fallen world as a form of chaos that will one day be replaced by a well-ordered cosmos. God will turn our present painful living east of Eden into a harmonious cosmos on the last day, when Christ returns to usher in the perfect Kingdom of God.

Conclusion

In this chapter we have seen that Jesus is fully engaged with the disorder in the world—in the diseases and ailments of humanity, and in the disruptive and dangerous powers of nature. His actions to alleviate human suffering and to remove dangerous threats to well-being reveal God's care and compassion for people and the world. But God's plans go well beyond this. Those who were healed eventually died. And storms at sea continued to take lives. Jesus' miracles were dramatic, but in and of themselves they were temporary fixes. But such actions were not the end or goal of Jesus' ministry. They were signs that he had come to heal the deeper wounds causing humanity's great and ongoing ills. As Son of Man he came as the human being God originally intended to rule over the creation. He came to reestablish true governance of the world, and thereby inaugurate the eternal kingdom of God. Infection diseases, caused by viruses, were a major aspect of the disorder that Jesus came to reorder. In these actions Jesus fulfills the responsibilities of man-made-in-the-image-of-God to subdue the earth and thereby exercise faithful dominion over God's creation (Genesis 1.26-28). Jesus reveals that he is the realization of the "one like a son of man" whose "dominion is an everlasting dominion that will not pass away, and his kingdom is one that will never be destroyed" (Daniel 7.13, 14).

6

JESUS DIES & RISES
Rescue Effected

Introduction

In the last chapter we saw that Jesus revealed his concern for the sick and dying by healing them. But we also saw that healing was not the final goal of his ministry. Healing and subduing the powerful forces of nature were signals that God was at work through Jesus rescuing the world from its corruption and certain death. We saw that these actions revealed his identity as the Son of Man and his mission of inaugurating the kingdom of God. In this chapter we look more deeply at the significance of Jesus' identity and mission. Who is this Son of Man and what is the kingdom of God?

The Son of Man in the Old Testament

Anyone who reads the Gospels soon discovers that Jesus repeatedly identified himself with the phrase or title "Son of Man". But what does this enigmatic phrase mean? The best way to grasp its meaning as Jesus used it is to recognize that he adopted it from the Old Testament Scriptures, the books he claimed spoke of him and explained his life and ministry. He said to those on the road to Emmaus: "O foolish ones, and slow of heart to believe all that the prophets have spoken! Was it not necessary that the Christ should suffer these things and enter into his glory?" And Luke tells us, "And beginning with Moses and all the Prophets he explained to them these matters about himself in all the Scriptures" (Luke 24.25-27). Jesus shaped his life and ministry around a mission he found in the Scriptures concerning one identified as the Son of Man. The phrase becomes particularly important when used in an end-time vision by Daniel the prophet. But earlier it had been used in the Psalms. We begin there.

The Son of Man in the Psalms:
Genuine Humanity

The Psalmist speaks of the "son of man" as he meditates upon the glorious creation of humanity in Genesis 1:

> What is man that you are mindful of him,
> The son of man that you care for him?
> You have made him a little lower than the angels,
> And crowned him with glory and honor.
> You have given him dominion over the works of your hands;
> You have put all things under his feet.
> (Psalm 8.4-6)

Here the parallelism indicates that the "son of man" is used synonymously with "man", that is, humanity. God crowned humanity, the son of man, with glory and honor, giving him dominion over his creation, the work of his hands. Likewise Psalm 90.3 refers to the "sons of men" when it reflects on the creation of man from the dust of the earth (cf. Genesis 2.7)

> You return humans to the dust,
> and say, "Return, O sons of men."

Interestingly, Jewish scholars would later translate Genesis 1.1 into Aramaic with a telling addition. In order to emphasize the emptiness of the pre-ordered creation in Genesis 1.1, the translators added "solitary of the sons of men"; that is, there were no humans.

> At the beginning the Lord created the heavens and the earth. And the earth was vacancy and desolation, solitary of the sons of men, and void of every animal, and darkness was upon the face of the abyss, and the Spirit of mercies from before the Lord breathed upon the face of the waters.
> (Targum Ps-Jon. Genesis 1.1)

These texts indicate that the basic meaning of the phrase "son of man" is human or humanity.

The initial "son of" makes emphatic the following noun. Thus, the "sons of the prophets" were prophets, regardless of their father's vocation (2 Kings 2.3, 5, 7, 15). While this idiom may sound odd to us, use of "son of ..." is common in the Old

Testament and was used to highlight the essential characteristic of the named noun. Because we do not use this idiom in English, our translations of the Bible usually hide its presence. For example, the phrase "sons of Belial" occurs frequently in the Old Testament, but the NIV translates this as troublemakers (Dt 13.13), wicked men (Judges 19.22; 20.13), scoundrels (1 Sam. 2.12; 10.27) or evil men (2 Sam. 23.6). Other examples abound: "Sons of might" are mighty men or fighters (2 Sam 17.10). A "son of murder" is a murderer (2 Kings 6.32). "Sons of singers" are musicians (Neh. 12.28). A "son of oil" is an anointed person (Zech. 4.14). A "son of one year" is a one year old (Ex. 12.5). A "son of a beating" is one found guilty of a crime and deserves a beating (Dt. 25.2). And a "son of affliction" is an afflicted or oppressed person (Proverbs 31.5). We can be thankful that the idiom is usually not translated literally, because it can be confusing to us when it is. For example, we read in 1 Samuel 20.30: "Then Saul's anger was kindled against Jonathan, and he said to him, 'You son of a perverse, rebellious woman!'" Saul was angry with Jonathan, not his mother! Thus, by understanding this idiom we recognize that a "son of man" is one who is in essential nature a human being. The New Revised Standard Version clarifies this by translating "son of man" as "human being" (Dan. 7.13) or "mortal" (Ps 8.4; 146.3) or something similar. But the phrase will take on greater meaning and significance as the purpose and plans of God to rescue the world are further developed. For example, in Psalm 80, the "son of man" is not just any human.

In Psalm 80.14-19 the idiom "son of man" takes on a more nuanced significance. The Psalmist is praying for the people of Israel, God's vine, because some disaster has overcome the nation: "Restore us, O God of hosts. Let your face shine so that we may be saved" (80.3, 7). He reminds God that He chose Israel to be His servant people: "You brought a vine out of Egypt, you drove out the nations and planted it. You cleared the ground for it and it took deep root and filled the land" (80.8). He then prays,

> Turn again, O God of hosts! Look down from heaven and behold, have regard for your vine, the stock your right hand planted, the son you made strong for yourself. . . . Let your hand be on the man of your right hand, the son of man whom you have made strong for yourself.
> (Psalm 80.14-15, 19)

The Psalmist, pleading with God to act on behalf of downtrodden Israel, reminds Him of the special care He showed to Israel in choosing them to be His unique covenant servant people to accomplish His plans to rescue the world. He describes Israel as God's "right hand man", God's "son", and "the son of man whom you made strong for yourself". When God rescued the children of Israel, the sons of Abraham, out of Egypt He called them "my son" (Exodus 4.22-23; cf. Hosea 11.1). This relationship between God and Israel gave them a unique identity in the world. The "right hand" was the place of honor (Ps 110.1; cf. Ps 8.5). As God's priestly kingdom (Exodus 19.6), they would mediate the message of God to the world, to all humanity, and display God's intentions for human society. God would work out his plans for the world and all humanity through the nation of Israel. Their distinctive calling meant they were to exemplify genuine humanity, hence they were "the son of man you made strong for yourself" (Psalm 80.19). The Aramaic Targum translates "son of man" here as "King Messiah," thus indicating that the king of Israel embodies and represents the whole nation. Whether one sees this as the king or the whole nation, it is evident that the son of man represents genuine humanity. Because humanity has fallen far from its calling, the nation of Israel, led by its king, is chosen to represent humanity in the service of God.

Thus, we see that the phrase "son of man" might be regarded as a circumlocution for "human being" or simply "human"; however, Adamic humanity, having chosen the wrong path in life, now suffering the corruptive consequences of its sins, is in a degenerative state, and is in danger of destroying itself altogether (Genesis 6.3, 5; Ps 14.1-3). But this state is not what God intended for humanity; this is a perversion of genuine humanity; and while the phrase "son of man" may at times reflect this degraded condition of mortal man (Numbers 23.19; Isaiah 51.12), it cannot be said to reflect the glorious intention of God. Therefore, the use of the phrase in such texts as Psalms 8 and 80 suggests that the idiom "son of man" is being used in a more honorable sense, harkening back to the original creation and calling of humanity, to suggest one who is chosen to restore that original glorious position of humanity and fulfill the plan of God.

The Son of Man in Daniel:
Humanity's Dominion Restored

Daniel's use of the phrase takes us further in the direction of fulfilling God's plans for his creation. The Daniel 7.13 reference to "one like a son of man" is generally regarded as the most important Old Testament passage influencing Jesus' understanding and use of the phrase. Daniel describes a vision of the rise and fall of the kingdoms of the world. In this summary review of the coming history of the world Daniel sees four kingdoms established by wicked rulers. They exercise their dominion by means of evil, injustice, violence, and oppression; therefore, these kings and their kingdoms are no longer worthy of being regarded as human. They have fallen to the level of the beasts, ruled by earthly or fleshly instincts rather than by a spiritual impulse. And so Daniel sees them as beasts. He writes,

> I saw in my vision by night . . . four great beasts came up out of the sea, different from one another. The first was like a lion and had eagles' wings. . . . The second was like a bear . . . and behold another, like a leopard . . . and after this, behold, a fourth beast, terrifying and dreadful and exceedingly strong. (Daniel 7.2-7)

Daniel is told specifically that "these great beasts are four kings" (7.17). Each is described as vicious and ruthless in its exercise of dominion. Daniel sees their kingdoms rise and fall. One by one "their dominion is taken away" by God (7.12). But then another figure appears in the vision:

> Behold, with the clouds of heaven there came one like a son of man. He came to the Ancient of Days and was presented before Him. And to him was given dominion and glory and a kingdom, that all peoples, nations, and languages should serve him. His dominion is an everlasting dominion, which shall not pass away, and his kingdom one that shall not be destroyed. (Daniel 7.13-14)

The rule of beastly kings has ended and a new kingdom is being established. This new kingdom is led by "one like a son of man"; that is, one who is human, not like one of the beasts who exercised dominion ruthlessly and wickedly. This one is a genuine representative of what God intended humanity to be from the beginning, and what Israel was called to be as God's covenant servant people. His kingdom will never end. His dominion is an everlasting dominion, and all other nations, people groups, and language groups will serve him.

All of this is clear. However, when Daniel is told the meaning of his vision there is a surprising twist. The "one like a son of man" is unexpectedly transformed from a single individual into a group, "the saints of the Most High God," who receive the eternal kingdom. How the one become the many is not explained. But this surprising transformation is spoken of no less than three times (7.18, 22, 27). In the last summary Daniel is once more told about the end of the fourth beast and the emergence of the eternal kingdom of the saints:

> His dominion shall be taken away, to be consumed and utterly destroyed. And the kingdom and the dominion and the greatness of the kingdoms under the whole heaven shall be given to the people, who are the saints of the Most High. His kingdom shall be an everlasting kingdom, and all dominions shall serve and obey him.
> (Daniel 7.26-27)

Daniel's vision is a very brief picture of the world that God intended when He created it and gave humanity stewardship of it. He sees humanity exercising proper dominion over His creation.

The vision renews hope that humanity will one day fulfill their calling to exercise proper stewardship over the earth in such a way as to enable it to achieve its potential. This brief excursion into the way the Old Testament uses the phrase "son of man" allows us to better understand why Jesus defined himself by this phrase.

Jesus' Identity as the Son of Man: Fulfilling Humanity's Vocation

We now return to the New Testament and the Gospels to learn more about Jesus and his identity as the Son of Man. As has been said, Jesus regularly identified himself with the phrase. An example of the significance of the title is found in the story of Jesus and Zacchaeus. Luke tells us that Zacchaeus "was a chief tax collector and was rich" (Luke 19.2). This brief but pointed description clearly reveals Zacchaeus to be a ruthless businessman, willing to exploit and oppress for his own gain. He illustrates what is wrong with humanity. He could easily be regarded as an example of the beastly nature of corrupted humanity. But this man encounters Jesus and is transformed. Luke tells us the story:

> Zacchaeus stood and spoke to the Lord. "Behold, Lord, the half of my goods I give to the poor. And if I have defrauded anyone of anything, I restore it fourfold." And Jesus said to him, "Today salvation has come to this house, since he also is a son of Abraham. For the Son of Man came to seek and to save the lost."
> (Luke 19.8-10)

Here Jesus says his mission as the Son of Man, the representative of humanity or the genuine human, is to save lost humanity, to restore humanity to its proper condition and to enable humanity to regain its proper place as stewards of God's world. Zacchaeus illustrates that transformation from a ruthless authority to a righteous steward, now exercising proper responsibility over his domain.

Another example of Jesus' identification of himself as the Son of Man occurs after he is betrayed and arrested and then appears before the High Priest who questions him about his identity:

> "I adjure you by the living God, tell us if you are the Messiah, the Son of God." Jesus said to him, "You have said so. But I tell you, from now on you will see the Son of Man seated at the right hand of power and coming on the clouds of heaven." Then the High Priest tore his robes and said, "He has uttered blasphemy. What further witnesses do we need?"
> (Matthew 26.63-65)

In his response to the High Priest, Jesus refers directly to Daniel's vision of one like a son of man coming on the clouds to receive an eternal kingdom, and claims that he is fulfilling that vision. Jesus is the human who ends the dominion of beastly rulers and kingdoms and inaugurates a righteous kingdom that will never end. Jesus begins actualizing the vision of Daniel, which had excited the hope and promise that God's intentions for creation through humanity's faithful stewardship would be realized.

The followers of Jesus later understood the meaning of these words, and they proclaimed the good news that after his death and resurrection Jesus ascended to the right hand of the Father (Romans 8.34; Ephesians 1.20; Hebrews 1.3 et al.), where he took his seat as ruler over earth and heaven (cf. Matthew 28.18). Stephen, as he was dying, had a vision of Jesus at the right hand of God, and cried out, "Behold, I see the heavens opened, and the Son of Man standing at the right hand of God" (Acts 7.56). Jesus' ascension was seen by the early church as a fulfillment of Psalm 110.1-2:

> The Lord said to my lord,
> Sit at my right hand,
> Until I make your enemies your footstool.
> The Lord sends forth from Zion
> Your mighty scepter.
> Rule in the midst of your enemies!

This psalm is referenced in the New Testament more frequently than any other Old Testament passage, thus revealing its importance to the early Christians for understanding the identity and mission of Jesus (e.g., Acts 2.34-36; 1 Cor. 15.25; Hebrews 1.13; et al.). Their Christological reading of this text was inspired by Jesus himself, who initiated its usage (Matthew 22.41-46). Thus, for the writers of the New Testament, Jesus, the Son of Man, the genuine human, is now exercising dominion over God's creation previewing the ultimate fulfillment of God's plans begun at creation. Jesus is doing in the real world what Daniel saw in vision. He is subduing and harnessing the world's powers, and cultivating and protecting its productive qualities, even in the midst of his enemies. Jesus is now fulfilling humanity's vocation as faithful stewards of the creation.

Jesus' Mission:
Inaugurating the Kingdom of God

If it is clear that Jesus' identity is summed up in the phrase "Son of Man", it is equally clear that his mission is summed up in the phrase "the kingdom of God." Mark tells us that Jesus' ministry begins with a grand announcement, "the good news," that the kingdom of God is at hand.

> After John was arrested, Jesus came into Galilee proclaiming the good news of God, saying, "The time is fulfilled and the kingdom of God is at hand! Turn and believe in the good news!"
> (Mark 1.14-15)

Jesus came to inaugurate the long-awaited Kingdom of God. In order to understand why the announcement of the kingdom was such good news, and why it was so eagerly anticipated, we need to consider the hope for such a kingdom as it is presented in the Old Testament. In order to understand why Jesus was rejected and killed it is also necessary to understand the kingdom message he preached and taught. The kingdom he invited others to join is at the heart of the Christians story.

The Kingdom of God in the Old Testament

By the time of Jesus the Jewish scholars and teachers had clarified their understanding of total history, their grand narrative—past, present, and future. They perceived all of history as divided into two eras or two ages or two worlds. The present age was an era in which evil, sin, and death reigned throughout the world. This era is exemplified by humanity's rejection of God in Genesis 3 and epitomized in the empires initiated by Nimrod, Assyria and Babylon (Genesis 10-11). But God had announced plans to rescue this world. The plan would result in the removal of all corruption and the establishment of justice and right in the age to come. The plan began with the choice of Abram and continued with the emergence of the nation of Israel.

The people of Israel were his special servant-nation chosen to display the wisdom of God's Law in constructing a just human society. By accepting God's kingship, as Adam had failed to do, they would manifest the kingdom of God and exercise faithful governorship. Tragically, however, Israel chose to rule like all the other nations and practice the same injustices. They too followed the path of Adam. In consequence of their failure, they were overtaken by Gentile empires and groaned under their exploitative and oppressive dominions.

Nevertheless, Israel looked forward to the day when God's chosen king would arrive. He would overthrow the unjust empires and inaugurate the righteous kingdom of God. At that time Israel would be liberated from idolatrous foreign rulers and reestablished as the triumphant manifestation of the kingdom of God. It would be an age of righteousness, justice, peace, and eternal life. The nations would recognize that God was with Israel and they would seek her wisdom and guidance. Isaiah pictures this future age:

> It shall come to pass in the latter days that the mountain of the house of the Lord shall be established as the

highest of the mountains, and shall be lifted up above the hills, and all the nations shall flow to it. Many peoples will come and say: "Let us go up to the mountain of the Lord, to the house of the God of Jacob, that he may teach us his ways, and that we may walk in his paths," for out of Zion shall go forth the Law, and the word of the Lord from Jerusalem.
(Isaiah 2.2-3)

In words that would later be taken up by John in his apocalyptic vision, Isaiah describes the coming kingdom as a complete transformation of the world, a new heaven and a new earth:

Behold, I create new heavens and a new earth, and the former things shall not be remembered or come into mind. Be glad and rejoice forever in that which I create; for behold I create Jerusalem to be a joy, and her people to be a gladness. I will rejoice in Jerusalem and be glad in my people. No more shall be heard in it the sound of weeping and the cry of distress.
(Isaiah 65.17-19)

The turn of the ages, from evil to good, would be accomplished in a period of time designated "the Day of the Lord." It was a day of judgment and salvation—judgment for the unrighteous who promote unjust practices, and salvation for the righteous who serve God faithfully. This decisive moment would terminate the old world, ending the reign of injustice and death. The righteous would be raised from the dead to enter into the kingdom and live with

God forever (Daniel 12.1-3). The kingdom would be characterized by righteousness, justice, and peace (*shalom*).

But while the Israelite leaders hoped for the coming of this kingdom, the prophets warned them that they would not escape judgment, because they themselves promoted oppressive and unjust practices. Israel's leaders were only deceiving themselves in their hopes that they would be the recipients of the kingdom of God. They ignored the reality that God's judgment in the Day of the Lord would necessarily condemn their evil behavior. They were not living in accordance with God's Law. They were not displaying the justice and mercy and love of God. Therefore, the Day of the Lord would be a time of judgment. Amos warns the leaders of Israel who oppress the poor and practice injustice:

> Woe to you who desire the Day of the Lord!
> Why would you have the Day of the Lord?
> It is darkness and not light,
> As if a man fled from a lion,
> Only to be met by a bear,
> Or went into a house and leaned his hand against a wall,
> and a serpent bit him.
> Is not the day of the Lord darkness and not light,
> Gloom with no brightness at all?
> (Amos 5.18-20)

Amos then reveals a new Israel would emerge on the other side:

> I will restore the fortunes of my people, Israel,
> And they shall rebuild the ruined cities and inhabit them;
> They shall plant vineyards and drink their wine,

They shall make gardens and eat their fruit.
I will plant them on their land,
And they shall never again be uprooted
out of the land I have given them.
(Amos 9.14-15)

Amos reveals that the people of God who survive judgment receive the ruins of the old city and rebuild it; they cultivate their gardens and eat their fruit, they plant vineyards and drink their wine. This new Israel, living in the kingdom, begins to fulfill their human vocation spelled out in Genesis 1-2: rule over, subdue, cultivate, care for the creation.

Isaiah wrote of the judgment against the arrogance of humanity:

For the Lord of hosts has a day
Against all that is proud and lofty,
Against all that is lifted up—
And it shall be brought low. . . .
The haughtiness of mankind shall be humbled,
And the lofty pride of humans shall be brought low,
And the Lord alone will be exalted in that day.
(Isaiah 2.12, 17)

Isaiah 2.4 describes the peace and harmony that prevail after judgment:

They shall beat their swords into plowshares,
And their spears into pruning hooks.
Nation shall not lift up sword against nation,
Neither shall they learn war anymore.

Isaiah's vision of the new world includes peace in the animal kingdom too:

> The wolf will live with the lamb,
> The leopard will lie down with the goat,
> The calf and the lion and the yearling together,
> And a little child shall lead them.
> The cow will feed with the bear,
> Their young will lie down together,
> And the lion will eat straw like the ox.
> The infant will play near the cobra's den,
> And the young child will put its hand into the viper's nest.
> They will neither harm nor destroy on all my holy mountain.
> For the earth will be filled with the knowledge of the Lord as
> waters cover the sea.
> (Isaiah 11.6-9; cf. Isaiah 65.25)

Isaiah says of the natural world, "The desert and parched land will be glad; the wilderness will rejoice and blossom. Like the crocus it will burst into bloom" (35.1-2). "The burning sand will become a pool, the thirsty ground bubbling springs" (35.7). In regard to humans he says, "Then the eyes of the blind and the ears of the deaf will be opened; then the lame will leap like a deer, and the mute tongue shout for joy" (35.5-6).

Zephaniah too prophesies judgment, extending his vision to the whole of humanity: "he will make a full and sudden end of all the inhabitants of the earth" (1.18) and "all the earth shall be consumed" (3.8).

The great Day of the Lord is near,
Near and hastening fast;
The sound of the day of the Lord is bitter;
The mighty man cries aloud there.
A day of wrath is that day,
A day of distress and anguish,
A day of ruin and devastation,
A day of darkness and gloom,
A day of clouds and thick darkness.
(Zephaniah 1.14-15)

But Zephaniah is hopeful, because he also sees a new humanity rising out of the ruins of the old world (3.9-13).

> For at that time I will change the speech of the peoples to a pure speech, that all of them may call upon the name of the Lord and serve Him with one accord. On that day you shall not be put to shame because of the deeds by which you have rebelled against me; for then I will remove from your midst your proudly exultant ones, and you shall no longer be haughty in my holy mountain. But I will leave in your midst a people humble and lowly. They shall seek refuge in the name of the Lord, those who are left in Israel. They shall do no injustice and speak no lies, nor shall there be found in their mouth a deceitful tongue. For they shall graze and lie down, and none shall make them afraid.

Zephaniah is here responding to an important question suggested by his vision of the totality of judgment in the Day of the Lord. If the whole of humanity is judged as rebellious (1.18; 3.8), where does the new humanity come from? Who is left to populate the world to come? For Zephaniah the judgment reveals a remnant of survivors (cf. 2.7, 9), who will be changed, forgiven, humbled, and who will no longer be arrogant and selfish, who no longer practice injustice or deceit.

These texts (and others) reveal that the prophets established a clear pattern for future history. Their grand narrative was well-known. God would first judge the sins of the world, and after that, and as a consequence of that, He would save a remnant, the faithful ones, who would inherit the eternal kingdom, the world to come. They would live in righteousness and peace, and in harmony with the natural world. The earth would produce an abundance of crops and the animal kingdom would live peaceably with all. Righteous Gentiles remaining after judgment would recognize Israel's God as the one true God and would come to Jerusalem to learn His ways. This prophetic literature shaped and prepared the minds of those who would eventually hear Jesus preach and teach.

Jesus and the Kingdom

When Jesus emerged from anonymity he announced, "The time is fulfilled, and the kingdom of God is at hand: return to God and believe this good news" (Mark 1.14-15). His statement in the synagogue in Nazareth at the beginning of his ministry was clear:

The scroll of the prophet Isaiah was given to him. He unrolled the scroll and found the place where it was written:

"The Spirit of the Lord is upon me,
because he has anointed me to proclaim good news
to the poor.
He has sent me to proclaim liberty to the captives
and recovery of sight to the blind,
to set at liberty those who are oppressed,
to proclaim the year of the Lord's favor."

He rolled up the scroll, gave it back to the attendant,
and sat down. The eyes of all in the synagogue were
fixed on him. And he began to speak to them, saying,
"Today, this Scripture is fulfilled in your hearing."
(Luke 4.18-21)

The claim was indeed remarkable. Jesus was announcing that he had been sent to bring into concrete reality what the prophets saw in hopeful visions, the age to come, the kingdom of God. Jesus then embarked on a ministry of powerful deeds—miracles—demonstrating that his words were trustworthy. He opened the eyes of the blind and the ears of the deaf; he made the lame leap like deer (Isaiah 35.5-6 and Matthew 15.30); he subdued the power of threatening storms on the Sea of Galilee (Mark 4.35-41); he transformed water into wine (John 2). John the Baptist sent his disciples to ask Jesus—"Are you the one who is to come, or should we look for another?" Jesus replied:

Go and tell John what you see and hear: the blind receive their sight and the lame walk, lepers are cleansed and the deaf hear, and the dead are raised up, and the poor have

good news preached to them. Blessed is the one who is not offended by me.
(Matthew 11.3-6)

Each of these dynamic acts was a sign that the kingdom of God, from the age to come, was penetrating the present age. Such proleptic incursions of the coming kingdom meant that the present age and its rulers were under threat. The kingdom Jesus declared and displayed in his ministry was advancing and would eventually undermine and overthrow all unjust kingdoms. War was inevitable. Great tribulation was coming. The Day of the Lord was at hand, judgment followed by salvation.

The officials and leaders of Israel recognized Jesus had great powers (John 3.2), but his stories often exposed their hypocrisy and condemned their behavior as characteristic of this present evil age and worthy of the judgment of God (Matthew 21.45). They realized Jesus identified them as the enemies of God who would be judged and destroyed in the great Day of Judgment. So they retaliated and claimed that his powers were demonic, not from God (Matthew 12.24). When Jesus learned this, he said,

Every kingdom divided against itself is laid waste, and no house or city divided against itself will stand. If Satan casts out Satan, he is divided against himself. How then will his kingdom stand? And if I cast out demons by Beelzebul, by whom do your sons cast them out? Therefore they will be your judges. But if it is by the Spirit of God that I cast out demons, then the kingdom has come upon you.
(Matthew 12.25-28)

At another time, some who opposed him asked when this kingdom would commence. He replied,

> The kingdom of God is not coming in ways that can be observed, nor will they say, "Look, here it is!" or "There!" for behold, the kingdom of God is in the midst of you! (Luke 17.20-21)

Jesus repeatedly taught his followers about the nature of this kingdom. It would not burst upon the scene, obvious to all, in a grand and undeniable form. Instead, it would emerge in an almost invisible manner, quietly and slowly growing, undetectable by natural sight. "The kingdom of God is like . . . a man who sowed seeds in a field, . . . a grain of mustard seed, . . . a treasure hidden in a field, . . . a merchant in search of a pearl, . . . a net thrown into the sea, . . ." (Matthew 18). Like a seed, the kingdom starts small but grows. Like treasure it must be sought diligently, but it can be found. It's right there in the midst of you, but you can't see it with physical eyes; you can only see it with spiritual eyes. Jesus continued planting seeds and instructed his disciples to do the same. In time the seeds would grow.

But antagonism toward Jesus and his message grew, the battle between the two kingdoms intensified, and Jesus was killed. His followers were devastated. "We hoped he was the one to redeem Israel" (Luke 24.21). Three days later he was with them again, having risen from death and entered into a new kind of life, eternal life. After forty days Jesus ascended to the right hand of God and began to rule over the kingdom he had inaugurated in his earthly ministry. Now it was his disciples who were responsible to cultivate the seed and see the kingdom grow. But in order to do that, they needed to understand what had happened. Why did he die? What was the meaning of this death? How could death serve the kingdom he preached?

Interpreting Jesus' Death

Steeped in the dire prophetic warnings of the Day of the Lord, his followers, perhaps surprisingly, interpreted the horrific death of Jesus as God's judgment on rebellious Israel and corrupt humanity. As Israel's Messiah he represented the nation before God—he embodied the nation that had chosen not to follow God. As the "Son of Man" Jesus represented Adamic humanity before God, in all their rebellious and evil ways. His death was the inevitable death of a world gone awry, a world built on lies. And his resurrection was the salvation of the faithful remnant in the Day of the Lord.

The Gospel writer Mark tells of the events surrounding the crucifixion of Jesus in such a way as to indicate his death was the fulfillment of the judgment aspect of the Day of the Lord. Mark writes, "When it reached noon there was darkness over the whole land [earth] for three hours. Jesus then cried out *'Eloi, Eloi, lema sabachthani'*, that is, My God, my God, why have you forsaken me?" (Mark 15.33). Mark is here aligning the death of Jesus with Amos' prophesy of judgment in the Day of the Lord: "And on that day, declares the Lord God, I will make the sun go down at noon and darken the earth in broad daylight. . . . I will make it like the mourning for an only son, and the end of it like a bitter day" (Amos 8.9-10). Dale C. Allison Jr. writes, "One concludes, therefore, that Mark 15:33, drawn up as it is in dependence upon Amos 8:9 sees in the historical crucifixion of Jesus the fulfillment of a prophesy concerned with the great Day of the Lord." (Allison 1985: 30). Herman Waetjen, who translates "son of man" as "New Human Being", explains the spiritual dynamics occurring in the scene:

> Ironically, therefore, it is Jesus' integrity as the New Human Being that determines his fate. By maintaining his identification with his fellow human beings, even his enemies, he becomes the target of God's wrath. The enshrouding darkness, the darkness that occurs "over the entire earth," signifies within the narrative world of the Gospel the cosmic judgment that is taking place. . . .
>
> By remaining true to his identity as the New Human Being and refusing to disassociate himself from his fellow human beings, although rejected by them and separated from them by crucifixion, he becomes their representative before God. Burdened, however, with their evil through identification with them, he is struck down and suffers the consequences of divine retribution intended for them. . . .
>
> Rejected and smitten by both God and humankind, he nevertheless cleaves to both as he absorbs their enmity. Consequently he becomes the bridge that unites them, the bridge that spans the nothingness of death and links human beings once more to the source of life and possibility. On the other hand, in his complete isolation from God and human beings he becomes the embodiment of the scapegoat who bears the human infection of sin into the oblivion of nothingness.
>
> (Waetjen 1989: 235-36)

The Apostle Paul develops and clarifies Mark's perspective, arguing that Jesus died as rebellious humanity, thereby saving humanity from having to face judgment. When he is raised from death, he emerges as the new human, having deposited humanity's sins in the grave. He gives humanity a new start. Those who identify themselves with Jesus, recognizing him as their head, and faithfully pursue his project to rescue the world, become a new humanity, building a new world, the kingdom of God, the new creation. Paul says: "Jesus gave himself for our sins to deliver us from the present evil age" (Galatians 1.4). "He has delivered us from the domain of darkness and transferred us to the kingdom of his beloved Son, in whom we have redemption, the forgiveness of sins" (Colossians 1.13-14). For Paul, Christ is the turning point of history, the end of the old world and the beginning of the new. God is at work through Jesus Christ starting a new creation. He writes to the Corinthians (2 Cor. 5.16-17):

> From now on, therefore, we regard no one from a human point of view; even though we once knew Christ from a human point of view, we know him no longer in that way. So if anyone is in Christ, there is a new creation; everything old has passed away; see everything has become new.

The Christian narrative has reached its decisive turning point. The world has changed. In the one man, Jesus Christ, God brought the old world to an end, and inaugurated the new world in his resurrection. The old humanity, Adamic humanity, comes to its necessary conclusion in Jesus' death, and a new humanity rises in

Jesus' resurrection. This is the seed of a new world, a new humanity, a new creation. The followers of Jesus unite with him in this new existence and invite others to join them and cultivate the new world, the kingdom, they inherit.

Conclusion

As the Son of Man Jesus represents humanity. In his ministry he fulfills humanity's vocation to govern the earth as God's steward. In his crucifixion he completes humanity's death march. In his ascension he realizes humanity's destination of ruling over God's creation. In his death, resurrection, and ascension to the right hand of God, Jesus effected the rescue of humanity and the world. This was the Day of the Lord. His death was the Day of Judgment on the debilitated world that humanity had constructed in its rejection of God. In his body he brought the world to its inevitable end. His resurrection was the Day of Salvation, giving humanity and the world a new beginning. The new creation had begun. His ascension to the right hand of God established humanity in its rightful place as stewards of God's creation. Jesus accomplished everything humanity had been created to do.

7

JESUS' FOLLOWERS
Rescue Progresses

Introduction

We have seen that the Christian narrative is optimistic. It portrays the ultimate fulfillment of God's creation project. According to Revelation 21-22 humanity will one day steward God's creation in such a way as to cultivate its potencies so that it flourishes brilliantly. Although one might look at the world today in a pessimistic way, and see corruption, decay, and death all around us—including the death caused by the coronavirus—the biblical narrative offers us a look at the world in a more hopeful way, and sees humanity progressing toward the goal of a renewed creation. An optimistic frame gives hope and encouragement to continue the quest to harness the natural realm; it draws us and beckons us into its reality. The new creation narrative reframes the coronavirus by revealing the ultimate success of humanity in restoring order to the cosmos. All service done for the kingdom of God today is not in vain, but will find its ultimate reward in its home in the new creation.

We currently live at some point between the inauguration and the consummation of the kingdom of God. Christ has begun the work of a new creation and a new humanity, but that work is not complete. The seed has been planted, but it needs to be nurtured in order to grow. And it has been growing. The optimistic outlook of Revelation 21-22 is supported by the evidence of real progress in history. Scientists currently working to understand the coronavirus can work hopefully, knowing their research is not in vain, but has and will move us forward to a time when we are able to subdue and harness the virus for good. It will be helpful and encouraging to describe some of the progress that has been made since Jesus Christ inaugurated the kingdom of God and began a new humanity. That is the purpose of this chapter.

God's Love for Humanity Revealed

In order to understand the progress that has been made, it will be helpful to reveal another aspect of the motivation that has inspired humans to seek that new creation reality. God's love for humanity is the foundation on which the new creation is built. Because God loves humanity He determined to rescue them from certain destruction and restore them to their intended position as stewards of creation. That love was manifest most brilliantly and effectively in Jesus Christ. He came to earth to rescue humanity and to restore the creation. He inaugurated that work through his life, death, resurrection, and ascension. He continues that work now through those who spread God's love and extend His kingdom around the world. Jesus taught his followers that God's love is revealed and transmitted through actions that redeem and restore humans from captivity to the social structures that result in death and destruction. Jesus describes the transfer of love from God to Jesus to the world through his followers.

As the Father has loved me, so have I loved you. Abide in my love. If you keep my commandments you will abide in my love, just as I have kept my Father's commandments and abide in his love. These things I have spoken to you that my joy may be in you, and that your joy may be full. This is my commandment, that you love one another as I have loved you. Greater love has no one than this, that someone lay down his life for his friends.
(John 15.9-12)

A new commandment I give to you, that you love one another. As I have loved you, so you are to love one another. By this all people will know that you are my disciples, if you have love for one another.
(John 13.34-35)

Jesus did not leave this teaching about love abstract. He made it concrete in one of his final lessons to his followers. He explained that when he returns to bring to completion the kingdom, all people will be judged. Some will enter the kingdom; others will not. Who will enter? Those who carried on his practice of loving service to those in need. They reveal by their imitation of Christ that they have been transformed by Christ and are now members of that new humanity that will inherit and steward the kingdom, the new creation. But those who remain unchanged by the message of Jesus, who were unconcerned for others, and who continued to support the social patterns that promoted exploitation, oppression, corruption and death, will not enter the kingdom. The message is powerful, so I quote it in full:

When the Son of Man comes in his glory, and all the angels with him, then he will sit on his glorious throne. Before him will be gathered all the nations, and he will separate people one from another as a shepherd separates the sheep and the goats. And he will place the sheep on his right, but the goats on his left. Then the King will say to those on his right, "Come, you who are blessed by my Father, inherit the kingdom prepared for you from the foundation of the world. For I was hungry and you gave me food, I was thirsty and you gave me drink, I was a stranger and you welcomed me, I was naked and you clothed me, I was sick and you visited me, I was in prison and you came to me." Then the righteous will answer him, saying, "Lord, when did we see you hungry and feed you, or thirsty and give you drink? And when did we see you a stranger and welcome you, or naked and clothe you? And when did we see you sick or in prison and visit you?" And the King will answer them, "Truly, I say to you, as you did it to one of the least of these my brothers, you did it to me."

Then he will say to those on the left, "Depart from me, you cursed, into the eternal fire prepared for the devil and his angels. For I was hungry and you gave me no food, I was thirsty and you gave me no drink, I was a stranger and you did not welcome me, naked and you did not clothe me, sick and in prison and you did not visit me." Then they will answer, saying, "Lord, when did we see you hungry or thirsty or a stranger or naked or sick or in prison and did not minister to you?" Then he will answer them, saying, "Truly, I say to you, as you did not do it to one of

the least of these, you did not do it to me." And these will go away into eternal punishment, but the righteous into life eternal.
(Matthew 25.31-46)

Jesus makes clear what his followers do, what God's love looks like when it is flowing through a human who has been restored and remade in God's image. The new humanity is revealed in its Jesus-like life choices, sacrificing self for the benefit of others. They will inherit the kingdom, which they will then steward for God. Those who continue to live in the old Adamic humanity, following the selfish social patterns that lead to destruction and death will realize that end. This teaching continued to motivate the followers of Jesus for centuries. For example, in the *Clementine Homilies* 11.4, written in 380 CE, we read:

> You are the image of the invisible God. Whence let not those who would be pious say that idols are the images of God, and therefore that it is right to worship them. For the image of God is man. He who wishes to be pious towards God does good to man, because the body of man bears the image of God. But all do not as yet bear his likeness, but the pure mind of the good soul does. However, as we know that man was made after the image and after the likeness of God, we tell you to be pious towards him, that the favor may be accounted as done to God, whose image he is. Therefore it behooves you to give honor to the image of God, which is man—in this way: food to the hungry, drink to the thirsty, clothing to the naked, care to

the sick, shelter to the stranger, and visiting him who is in prison, to help him as you can.

(cf. *Ps-Clementine Recognitions* 5.23)

God's Love for Humanity:
Health Care for All Humans

Christians were not the first to minister to the sick or to practice medicine, but they were the first to promote a ministry of medical care to all people without regard to social situation. Since Christians saw all humans as made in the image of God and as loved by God, they believed that all humans deserved to be cared for. They regarded health care as a human right, and therefore studied medicine and offered their services to all people. Christians did not limit health care to praying for the sick or seeking supernatural intervention, miraculous healing. They believed that God gave humans the ability and responsibility to understand the healing powers of the earth and to practice medicine. While doctors were available to the elite members of Greek and Roman society, the poor had no access to health care until Christianity began to express God's love to all people. Gary Ferngren writes:

> The concept of the church's care of "the poor" was basic to the founding of the earliest hospitals. The hospital was, in origin and conception, a distinctively Christian institution, rooted in Christian concepts of charity and philanthropy. There were no pre-Christian institutions in the ancient world that served the purpose that Christian hospitals were created to serve, that is, offering charitable

aid, particularly health care, to those in need. None of the
provisions for health care in classical times that have been
suggested as early exemplars—military and slave
infirmaries (*valetudinaria*), temples of Asclepius (*asclepieia*),
physicians' clinics (*iatreia*), or public physicians (*archiatri*)
—resembled hospitals as they developed in the late fourth
century.
(Ferngren 2009: 124)

The idea that God had infused the natural world with healing
powers was well-established in the Judaism that Christianity
emerged from. The *Wisdom of Ben Sira (Ecclesiasticus)* 38.1-15 (c. 180
BCE) reveals the attitude toward medicine and healing that
prevailed within Hellenistic Judaism and Christianity:

Make friends with the doctor, for he is essential to you;
God has also established him in his profession.
From God the doctor has his wisdom,
and from the king he receives sustenance.
Knowledge makes the doctor distinguished,
and gives access to those in authority.
God makes the earth yield healing herbs
which the prudent should not neglect;
was not the water sweetened by a twig,
so that all might learn his power?
He endows people with knowledge,
to glory in his mighty works,
through which the doctor eases pain,
and the druggist prepares his medicines.
Thus God's work continues without cease

in its efficacy on the surface of the earth.
My son, when you are ill, do not delay,
but pray to God, for it is he who heals.
Flee wickedness and purify your hands;
cleanse your heart of every sin.
Offer your sweet-smelling oblation and memorial,
a generous offering according to your means.
Then give the doctor his place
lest he leave; you need him too,
for there are times when recovery is in his hands.
He too prays to God
that his diagnosis may be correct
and his treatment bring about a cure.
Whoever is a sinner before his Maker
will be defiant toward the doctor.

Ben Sira is dependent on Genesis 1-2 for this perspective. He views humans as responsible to God for learning how the natural world works in order to provide healing cures. He recognizes that God commissions humans to the medical vocation and gives them the intelligence necessary to understand his mighty works in creation. He alludes to Genesis 1.11-12 when he writes "God makes the earth yield healing herbs." And he offers an example from Exodus 15.23-25 of a twig empowered by God to sweeten bitter waters. As Skehan and DiLella explain,

he implies that the "twig" had of itself, by God's design, the ability to make the bitter water fresh. Thus, "people might learn [God's] power" in creating such wood. … The point of 38.8bc is that "God's creative work"—i.e., the

"healing herbs" whose nature comes from the Lord— never ceases to do what God has ordained for it. Thus in sickness one should not despise or refuse these herbs but make use of them, since God created them precisely for healing. In vv 6-8 Ben Sira encourages further study to discover other plants and herbs with medicinal power: the God of nature has endowed human beings with the ability to learn the mysteries of nature in order to alleviate sickness and pain.
(Skehan and DiLella 1987: 442)

Skehan and DiLella (1987: 439) summarize: "Ben Sira singles out the practice of medicine for that high place in religious and civic affairs alike which doctors came to occupy among both Jews and Christians in the Near East in the centuries that were to follow."

The Christian theologian Origen, writing c. 240 CE, echoes this same perspective. He taught that "the science of medicine is useful and necessary for humanity" (*Contra Celsum* 3.12). In his homily on Psalm 37 Origen said, "God, who created the human body, knew the fragility of the human body, that it was weak and susceptible to sickness . . . and therefore he created medicine and delivered to men the science of medicine." (Psalm 37.1.1; J. P. Migne *Patrologiae Graeca* 12.13269). When commenting on King Asa's infirmity (1 Kings 15.23) Origen looks back to the creation account in Genesis 1 to highlight the important role of physicians in God's world. He argues that the physician's medical knowledge illustrates the God-ordained harmony of creation. Humans cultivate the earth for healing benefits to mankind. Origen argues that just as God gifts the earth with potencies to produce vegetation, so he gifts humanity with an intellect to understand the usefulness of these potencies for medicine. He alludes to Genesis 1.11-12 when he says that the creation is empowered by a divine word so that vegetation springs forth from the earth, and he combines this with an allusion to Genesis 1.28 when he says that physicians are stewards of God. [Origen, *Adnotationes in librum III regum 15.23;* J. P. Migne, *Patrologiae Graeca* 17.54-55].

God's Love for Humanity:
Health Care for All Humans in Church Practice

The Christian church emerged at a time in the history of the Roman Empire when disease was becoming particularly problematic. The increase in cities and global commerce contributed to the spread of infectious diseases. In the 2nd and 3rd centuries CE Christianity was an illegal religion, yet because of its care for the sick and dying it gained widespread respect and appreciation. By the early 4th century CE it had won over the Empire. Daniel Reff describes the environment in which Christianity grew:

> People were sicker and died prematurely in greater numbers during late antiquity and the early Middle Ages, as compared with the earlier reign of Augustus. As detailed later, smallpox, measles, plague, and malaria devastated Europe during the early Christian era and the subsequent early Middle Ages. Christianity provided a belief system as well as rituals to deal with disease and its profound consequences. Beginning with the earliest *ekklesiae,* and continuing with the rise of monasticism during the fourth

century, the Church made charity, particularly care of the sick and orphans central ministries of priests and monks. In what essentially was a disease environment, *ekklesiae* and monasteries functioned as centers for organizing and reorganizing lives that were shattered by epidemic disease as well as migration, warfare, and social unrest.
(Reff 2004: 37-38)

Historians have repeatedly demonstrated that the modern hospital has its origins in Christians practicing care of the sick. Often described as the first hospital, the Basiliad on the border of the city of Caesarea, was a huge complex of ministries that originated as a monastery dedicated to serving the poor and needy in Caesarea. The Basiliad was named after its founder Basil (330-379 CE), one of the Cappadocian Fathers. Basil grew up in a very wealthy family. Later he converted some of the family property into a monastery. But Basil's vision was for much more. He saw his monastery as an opportunity to serve people and provide for all their needs.

In about 356 CE Basil wrote the rules for the monastery and answered a series of questions for those who wondered if such extensive services were intrinsic to the Christian gospel. One of those questions, number 55, asked if providing medicine was a godly practice. He answered:

Each of the arts is God's gift to us, remedying the deficiencies of nature, as, for example, agriculture, since the produce which the earth bears of itself would not suffice to provide for our needs; the art of weaving, since the use of clothing is necessary for decency's sake and for

protection from wind; and similarly, for the art of building. The same is true, also of the medical art. Inasmuch as our body is susceptible to various hurts, some attacking from without and some from within by reason of the food we eat, and since the body suffers affliction from both excess and deficiency, the medical art has been vouchsafed us by God, who directs our whole life, as a model for the cure of the soul, to guide us in the removal of what is superfluous and in the addition of what is lacking. . . .
Now, the herbs which are the specifics for each malady do not grow out of the earth spontaneously; it is evidently the will of the Creator that they should be brought forth out of the soil to serve our need. Therefore, the obtaining of that natural virtue which is in the roots and flowers, leaves, fruits, and juices, or in such metals or products of the sea as are found especially suitable for bodily health, is to be viewed in the same way as the procuring of food and drink. . . . Consequently, we must take great care to employ this medical art, if it should be necessary, not as making it wholly accountable for our state of health or illness, but as redounding to the glory of God and as a parallel to the care given the soul. . . . When the favor of a cure is granted us, whether by means of wine mixed with oil, as in the case of the man who fell among the robbers [Luke 10.34], or through figs, as with Hezekiah [2 Kings 20.7], we are to receive it with thanksgiving.
(St Basil, *The Longer Rule*, Rule 55)

At the center of the community was the monastery, but in time it grew to include a soup kitchen to feed the poor, an orphanage, an education center for teaching trades, clothing for the poor, housing for travelers, and a hospital with professional medical personnel.

After his death, Basil's friend Gregory of Nazianzus, Archbishop of Constantinople, eulogized him, highlighting his work to provide medical treatment for the sick, and food and clothing for the poor: "Basil's care was for the sick, and the relief of their wounds, and the imitation of Christ, by cleansing lepers, not by a word, but in deed." Gregory described the Basiliad as "the new city, the storehouse of piety" supported by "the common treasury of the wealthy . . . freed from the power of the moth . . . and the corruption of time." According to Gregory, this magnificent new work was greater by far than those monuments typically identified as mankind's greatest achievements: the pyramids, the colossus of Rhodes, the mausoleum at Halicarnassus, the walls of Babylon, which offer nothing more than fame to their builders. For Gregory the Basiliad was "the most wonderful of all" because it served and dignified humanity.

> There is no longer before our eyes that terrible and piteous spectacle of men who are living corpses, the greater part of whose limbs have mortified, driven away from their cities and homes and public places and fountains, aye, and from their own dearest ones, . . . they are no longer the objects of hatred.

Gregory said that Basil impressed upon all the need to regard all humans with dignity.

> He took the lead in pressing upon men that they ought not to despise their fellow men, nor to dishonor Christ, the

one Head of all, by their inhuman treatment; but instead to take the misfortunes of others as opportunity of firmly establishing their own lot. . . . And thus, although of noble ancestry, he did not disdain to honor with his lips those diseased, but saluted them as brethren, not as some might think from vainglory, but as a consequence of his philosophy, and so giving silent instruction.
(Gregory of Nazianzus, *Oration* 43, section 63)

Another example of Christianity's care for the sick concerns the first hospital in Rome. This was established by a Christian woman named Fabiola. She was an extremely wealthy and powerful woman, a member of the Fabia family, the Roman ruling class. She was converted to Christianity through the ministry of Jerome. They became close friends, and after her death he eulogized her. His eulogy was then transcribed in a letter to her relative Oceanus (Jerome, *Letter* 77). Jerome describes her repentance in much detail. He then goes on to describe her transformed life:

Instead therefore of re-embarking on her old life, she broke up and sold all that she could lay hands on of her property (it was large and suitable to her rank), and turning it into money she laid out this for the benefit of the poor. She was the first person to found a hospital, into which she might gather sufferers out of the streets, and where she might nurse the unfortunate victims of sickness and want. Need I now recount the various ailments of human beings? Need I speak of noses slit, eyes put out, feet half burnt, hands covered with sores? Or of limbs dropsical and atrophied? Or of diseased flesh alive with worms?

Often did she carry on her own shoulders persons infected with jaundice or with filth. Often too did she wash away the matter discharged from wounds, which others, even though men, could not bear to look at. She gave food to her patients with her own hand, and moistened the scarce breathing lips of the dying with sips of liquid.

Jerome grounds such virtuous practices in the Christian vision of humanity, in the recognition that all humans are siblings and should care for one another. He writes:

> The poor wretch whom we despise, whom we cannot so much as look at, and the very sight of whom turns our stomach, is human like ourselves, is made of the same clay as we are, is formed of the same elements. All that he suffers we too may suffer. Let us then regard his wounds as though they were our own, and then all our insensibility to another's sufferings will give way before our pity for ourselves.

Conclusion

The story of the progress of health care and hospitals has been told in great detail elsewhere, so it is not necessary to continue that here. It will be helpful, however, to remind ourselves of the great progress that has been made. Scientists have continued to understand better the cause and cure of disease. The practice of variolation led to the discovery of vaccination, which has saved millions of lives. Smallpox provides an example of the effectiveness of vaccination against disease. This one disease has devastated human lives since before the time of Christ. The first known victim of smallpox is Pharaoh Ramses V (died 1157 BCE). Over the many centuries it spread across the globe the mortality rate for those infected was approximately 30%. In the two and half centuries prior to the discovery of the smallpox vaccine, William Guy estimated that the disease was responsible for 7.6% (1 in 13) of all deaths in London (Guy 1882: 399). After Edward Jenner discovered an effective vaccination, and convinced the government of its potential (c. 1800), the rate of deaths declined rapidly. In 1959 the World Health Organization (WHO) announced plans to eradicate the disease from the earth. Progress was slow in the early years, but renewed efforts beginning in 1967 brought significant results, so that on 8 May 1980 WHO announced that the world is free from smallpox. In 1988 the Global Polio Eradication Initiative was announced. Since that time the number of polio cases has been reduced by 99%. We are near to eliminating polio from the world.

Healthcare for the masses is now regarded by almost all nations and people as a basic human right. The teachings of Jesus about human dignity and worth have reached around the globe and are being practiced by many people and nations, many of whom do not know the origins of their belief and practice. All of the selfless acts of service by health care workers and other essential workers during the current coronavirus pandemic have followed in the path laid down by Jesus and contribute to the eternal kingdom he rules over.

CONCLUSION

The window of Christianity reveals the coronavirus pandemic to be a very serious threat to life and health, highlighting the dangers of nature untamed. But it also reveals that humanity will someday succeed in taming this virus. Such optimism should motivate people to cooperate in efforts to contain the virus and eradicate the disease. These efforts begin with scientific research and applications. Christianity's role is to support and encourage cooperation and selfless service to others.

The study of the natural world in order to employ its potencies for the benefit of humanity is both a scientific and religious endeavor. Looking through the window of Christianity one sees that scientific study of the world is a God-given responsibility to humanity for the enrichment and flourishing of the earth and of all living things. There is a natural harmony between religion and science. However, that window also reveals humanity's tendencies toward selfishness and greed, which can then lead to a disharmony between religion and science. Religion can and should be a positive influence on scientific research and activity by redirecting humanity's motives toward the improvement of others lives. But at times religion has had a negative influence on science; its beliefs were allowed to over-regulate the methods and outcomes of scientific research. Likewise, science can and should be a positive influence on religious practice by enabling humans to care for one another more effectively. But at times science has also demonstrated a negative tendency to make unwarranted religious claims. When each functions in a flawed manner, disharmony reigns, and each seeks to overwhelm the other in a totalitarian manner: religion dictates scientific results; science dictates religious beliefs. The history of the relationship between science and religion has been complicated. However, when working harmoniously religion undergirds science with foundational beliefs that the natural world functions with regularity and can be understood by the human mind. Science likewise provides religion with means of human flourishing.

The coronavirus pandemic presents a situation where harmony between religion and science is critically important. Each should support the other for the best outcome. The window of Christianity reframes the pandemic in an optimistic light, revealing that when harmony prevails in the relationship, a positive outcome can be expected. However, the history of the relationship reveals the potential for problems if disharmony between the two prevails. Therefore, religious believers should support scientific research and promote the advice of scientists. Scientists should be encouraged with the reassurance that their efforts are inspired and assisted by divine design and blessed by religious institutions.

Christians, as those who claim to order their lives by the Christian story, ought to be on the front lines of the effort to contain the virus and eradicate the disease. And many Christians are indeed acting selflessly and sacrificially in this effort, serving humanity as essential workers, healthcare workers, and in other ways that support human society. There are others who do not claim to be Christian in their beliefs, but who are equally compelled to that same selfless and sacrificial labor for the benefit of humanity. Such altruistic behavior fulfills our human responsibility announced in Genesis 1-2 and exemplified in the teachings and practice of Jesus Christ. All such efforts contribute to the ultimate success of the grand narrative. This cooperative activity reflects a deeper reality at work in the world. God is working through all such acts to bring to completion the rescue He effected in the death, resurrection, and ascension of Jesus Christ. The Christian values undergirding such acts (e.g., the dignity of all humans) have increasingly become the accepted norm in our world, regardless of our consciousness of those values. Many who do not confess Jesus Christ as Lord have nevertheless been influenced by his teachings and practice and therefore contribute to his mission.

Tom Holland's *Dominion: How the Christian Revolution Remade the World* argues that Christianity has revolutionized the world, despite the fact that most people alive today are barely aware of it. Christian values shape our institutions and practices to a remarkable degree. He concludes the book with this thought:

> Christianity, it seemed, had no need of actual Christians for its assumptions still to flourish. . . . As it was, the retreat of Christian belief did not seem to imply any necessary retreat of Christian values. Quite the contrary. Even in Europe – a continent with churches far emptier than those in the United States – the trace elements of Christianity continued to infuse people's morals and presumptions so utterly that many failed even to detect their presence. Like dust particles so fine as to be invisible to the naked eye, they were breathed in equally by

everyone: believers, atheists, and those who never paused so much to think about religion.

Christianity—the grand narrative described from Genesis to Revelation—marches on, progressing toward its consummation, whether or not we are aware of it. But to be aware of it provides us with an optimism that encourages us to work with greater cooperation, diligence, and hope, knowing that our efforts are not in vain, but will ultimately succeed.

FURTHER READING

Others have also written to provide a Christian perspective on the coronavirus pandemic. I recommend Walter Brueggemann's *Virus as a Summons to Faith: Biblical Reflections in a Time of Loss, Grief, and Uncertainty* (Eugene: Cascade 2020), and N. T. Wright's, *God and the Pandemic. A Christian Reflection on the Coronavirus and its Aftermath* (London: SPCK 2020).

Terence Fretheim's *Creation Untamed* provides a scholarly and accessible study of the creation account, explaining how the narrative reveals the natural world to be both good and dangerous. For those wanting a more thorough-going study of the relation between God, humanity, and nature, Fretheim offers *God and the World in the Old Testament, A Relational Theology of Creation* (Abingdon 2005).

Gary Ferngren has written several helpful works on the history of Christianity's impact on health care. His *Medicine and Health Care in Early Christianity* (Baltimore: John Hopkins UP 2009) is an excellent place to begin. Carl Zimmer's *A Planet of Viruses* (University of Chicago 2015) provides a great introduction to the topic of viruses and virology.

Those interested in exploring the idea that Christianity is progressively transforming human culture should read Tom Holland's *Dominion: How the Christian Revolution Remade the World* (London: Little, Brown 2019) and Nick Spencer's *The Evolution of the West* (London: SPCK 2016).

BIBLIOGRAPHY

Allison, Dale C. Jr. 1985. *The End of the Ages has Come*. Philadelphia: Fortress.

Brooke, John Hedley. 1991. *Science and Religion. Some Historical Perspectives*. Cambridge University Press.

Brueggemann, Walter. 2020. *Virus as a Summons to Faith. Biblical Reflections in a Time of Loss, Grief, and Uncertainty*. Eugene: Cascade.

Burnet, Frank MacFarlane. 1953. *Viruses and Man*. Melbourne: Penguin Books.

Davies, Stevan. 2014. *Spirit Possession and the Origins of Christianity*. Dublin: Bardic Press.

Delwart, Eric. 2016. "Viruses of the Human Body." *The Scientist*.

Ehrman, Bart. 2003. *The Apostolic Fathers, volume II*. Loeb Classical Library. Harvard University Press.

Ferngren, Gary. 2009. *Medicine and Health Care in Early Christianity*. Baltimore MD: Johns Hopkins University Press.

Foulongne, Vincent, et al. 2012. "Human Skin Microbiota." *PLoS ONE* 7(6).

Fretheim, Terence E. 2005. *God and the World in the Old. A Relational Theology of Creation.* Nashville TN: Abingdon.

Fretheim, Terence E. 2010. *Creation Untamed. The Bible, God, and Natural Disasters.* Grand Rapids MI: Baker Academic.

Greidanus, Stephen. 2018. *From Chaos to Cosmos.* Wheaton: Crossway.

Griffiths, Paul. 1999. "Time to Consider the Concept of Commensal Virus? *Reviews in Medical Virology.* 9:73-74.

Guy, William A. 1882. "Two Hundred and Fifty Years of Small Pox in London." *Journal of the Statistical Society of London* 45.3, pp. 399-443.

Heffernan, Thomas J. 2012. *The Martyrdom of Saints Perpetua and Felicity.* Oxford University Press.

Holland, Tom. 2019. *Dominion: How the Christian Revolution Remade the World.* London: Little, Brown.

Jonson, Albert. 2000. *A Short History of Medical Ethics.* Oxford University Press.

Liu, L. et al. 2019. "Commensal Viruses Maintain Intestinal Intraepithelial Lymphocytes via Noncanonical RIG-I Signaling." *Nature Reviews Immunology.* 20.1681-1691.

Margulis, Lynn. 1998. *Symbiotic Planet.* New York: Basic Books.

Mathewson, C. D. 2009. "Molecular Exploration of the First Century *Tomb of the Shroud* in Akeldama, Jerusalem." *PLoS ONE* 4(12).

Meier, John. 1990. "Jesus" in *The New Jerome Biblical Commentary*. Edited by Raymond Brown et al. Englewood Cliffs, NJ: Prentice-Hall, pp. 1316-1328.

Meyers, Eric and Carol L. Meyers. 2015. "Meiron in Upper Galilee" in *Galilee in the Late Second Temple and Mishnaic Periods, volume 2. The Archaeological Record from Cities, Towns and Villages* edited by David A. Fiensy and James R. Strange. Minneapolis: Fortress, pp. 379-388.

Mietzsch, Mario and Mavis Agbandie-McKenna. 2017. "The Good that Viruses Do." *Annual Review of Virology* 4.3-5.

Minton, K. 2019. "Commensal Viruses Contribute to Gut Health." *Nature Reviews Immunology*. 19.721.

Mitchell, Piers D. 2016. "Intestinal Parasites in the Crusades: Evidence for Disease, Diet, and Migration," in Adrian J. Boas, editor, *The Crusader World*. London: Routledge.

Moberly, R. W. L. 2009. *The Theology of the Book of Genesis*. Cambridge University Press.

Moule, C. F. D. 1964. *Man and Nature in the New Testament. Reflections on Biblical Ecology*. The Ethel M. Wood Lecture delivered before the University of London on 9 March 1964. London: The Athlone Press.

Mumcuouglu, K. Y., and J Zias, et al. 2003. "Body louse remains in textiles excavated at Masada, Israel," *Journal of Medical Entomology* 40, pp. 585-87

Nagar, Yossi and Flavia Sonntag. 2008. "Byzantine Period Burials in the Negev," *Israel Exploration Journal* 58 (90), pp. 79-93.

Pradeu, Thomas. 2016. "Mutualistic Viruses and the Heteronomy of Life." *Studies in History and Philosophy of Biological and Biomedical Sciences*. 59.80-88.

Reed, Jonathan. 2010. "Instability in Jesus' Galilee: A Demographic Perspective." *Journal of Biblical Literature* 129.2, pp. 343-365.

Reed, Jonathan. 2014 "Mortality, Morbidity, and Economics in Jesus' Galilee," *Galilee in the Late Second Temple and Mishnaic Periods: Life, Culture and Society* Volume 1. Edited by David A. Fiensy and James R. Strange. Minneapolis: Fortress, pp. 242-252.

Reff, Daniel. 2005. *Plagues, Priests, and Demons*. Cambridge University Press.

Risse, Guenter B. 1999. *Mending Bodies, Saving Souls*. Oxford University Press.

Rohrbaugh, Richard. 1996. *The Social Sciences and New Testament Interpretation*. Peabody MA: Hendrickson.

Roossinck, Marilyn. 2005. "Symbiosis Versus Competition in the Evolution of Plant RNA Viruses." *Nature Reviews Microbiology* 3.917-924.

Roossinck, Marilyn. 2011. "The Good Viruses: Viral Mutualistic Symbioses." *Nature Reviews Microbiology* 9.99-108.

Roossinck, Marilyn. 2015. A New Look at Plant Viruses and their Potential Beneficial Roles in Crops. *Molecular Plant Pathology* 16.4.331-333.

Roossinck, Marilyn. 2016. *Virus. An Illustrated Guide to 101 Incredible Microbes*. Princeton University Press.

Sarna, Nahum. 1989. *Genesis Commentary*. The JPS Commentary. Philadelphia: JPS.

Skehan, Patrick, and Alexander A. DiLella. 1987. *The Wisdom of Ben Sira*. The Anchor Bible. New York: Doubleday.

Spencer, Nick. 2016. *The Evolution of the West*. London: SPCK.

Waetjen, Herman C. 1989. *A Reordering of Power. A Socio-Political Reading of Mark's Gospel.* Minneapolis: Fortress Press.

Warnock, J. N. et al. 2011. "Introduction to Viral Vectors." *Methods in Molecular Biology* 737: 1-25

Westermann, Claus. 1971. *Creation.* London: SPCK.

Wynne, J. W. and L. F. Wang. 2013. "Bats and Viruses: Friend or Foe?" *PLoS Pathogens* 9.

Zimmer, Carl. 2015. *A Planet of Viruses.* 2nd edition. University of Chicago Press.